# The Evenings I Cried

## Havaskhan Kamchieva

© Havaskhan Kamchieva
## The Evenings I Cried
by: Havaskhan Kamchieva
Edition: June '2024
Publisher:
*Taemeer Publications LLC* (Michigan, USA / Hyderabad, India)

ISBN 978-93-5872-250-5

© **Havaskhan Kamchieva**

| | | |
|---|---|---|
| Book | : | The Evenings I Cried |
| Author | : | Havaskhan Kamchieva |
| Editor | : | Nilufar Rukhillayeva |
| Publisher | : | Taemeer Publications |
| Year | : | '2024 |
| Pages | : | 144 |
| Title Design | : | *Taemeer Web Design* |

*I dedicate this book to the loving memory of my mother Risolathon Ortiqboy kizi*

**Havaskhan Kamchieva**

Dilbar, who woke up from shouts, was staring at his father, mother and brother with sleepy eyes. "What are they quarrelling for again? Tears came to Dilbar's eyes, who was heartbroken by such quarrels. The girl, who had just turned twelve years old, was heartbroken to hear the noises in the house. After hearing his brother's words about the money, Dilbar realized what was the matter and began to plead with his brother, "My dear brother, no need to quarrel, here, in my folder, I have five soums of money that I have collected for books. Take that." Hearing this, her mother cried out, holding poor Dilbar to her. "Don't you feel sorry for this child? She cleaned the cocoon in the cocoon factory to buy books and notebooks and earned this money. What did you do as a brother or a father for her? You are dishonest! She is still a child? Don't touch her money...!" The mother's words stuck in her throat. His brother didn't care a bit, took the money from Dilbar and went out. "That's ok, don't cry, mom...," said Dilbar, who was nearly to cry. At that moment, the girl's heart was filled again as she realized that her father was also drunk. She bowed her head and sobbed. "Oh God! What is her mother guilty of? Why is she in such pain? Neither my father nor my brother understands her. It is hard for my poor mother," Dilbar knew how much pain her mother had suffered between two of them. In the morning, Dilbar woke up with swollen eyes. To help her mother, she cleaned and swept the yard. Then she took the bottles of wine her father had drunk the night before and threw them in the garbage. Then she went to work in the cocoon factory without even having breakfast. When she arrived, one of the employee women of the cocoon factory was sorting the girls and releasing young ones from work. "Now the cocoons are going to be cleaned on the higher shelves, those places are dangerous for you," he said, "You can go home now." After seven or eight girls had left, Dilbar came up slowly to the employee and said, My dear sister, I can't stop working. I need to get school supplies. Please help," she begged. An elderly woman who heard this said, "Umidakhon, help this girl, find a job suitable for her age." Seeing the tears in Dilbar's eyes, the employee got astonished, felt sorry for the girl, "Okay, you will pick up cocoons that are spilled around into a bucket. "You can't go to the upper shelves."Dilbar was Happy, "Thank you my dear sister!" she said, hastily wiping her tears. Distracted by work, Dilbar was not happy when it was time to go home in the evening and going home she watched the laughing older girls with envy. "They are happy, there are no quarrels and disorders in their places, how happy they are. What about us...? Always a quarrel. Only my mother is suffering from these quarrels. What if there is another one today?" Dilbar, who came through the gate with dreams, saw his father lying on the bed - and was humiliated. It was as if something broke from inside her. "Oh, my father, he's drunk again." But her mother was nowhere to be seen. "Where is my poor mom?"

"She calmed down a little when she crossed the threshold of the house and saw her mother. Dilbar, who came to her senses from her mother's voice saying, "Are you at home, my daughter," stared sadly into his mother's eyes. "Yes, I am...," she managed to say. Dilbar was sure to cry if her poor mother said anything. Realizing that, she walked towards the door barely holding herself together. She went to the shade of an apricot tree on the edge of the yard and began to wipe her painful tears. These were tears coming from the bottom of Dilbar's heart. She was trying to keep it together.However, she could not. It was like she was full of pain. For that reason, she sat for a long time. As dusk came, she got up slowly and entered the house. She looked at the mirror, wiped out her eyes red with tears and came up to her mother.

Risolat aya[1] said, "Where have you been, my daughter?" She turned to Dilbar and saw her daughter's eyes red from crying, and was crushed inside. At that moment, she wanted to say something to her daughter. But she swallowed her words seeing Dilbar's condition. Dilbar silently laid the table in front of his mother and put the kettle on the stove. While they were having tea together, her brother came. The girl, who was afraid of everything by constant quarrels, immediately stood up.

"Don't you have any meal? Only tea and bread again?" shouted his brother. "Brother, I'm just going cook it. Have some tea," said Dilbar, went out into the yard and came up to the hearth. "O God! At least today, may we spent in peace one day." Maybe the poor girl's cry reached God, anyway, her brother and father ate the meal cooked by Dilbar in silence.Before long, it was almost August. Everyone was busy buying school clothes and school supplies. Risolat aya was struggling to get a school uniform for her daughter. At that moment, her brother Madaminjon came in. Seeing her brother, Risolat's eyes were filled with tears. "How are you, brother, are you doing well?" she asked. "Sister, are you all right? Why are you crying?" asked her brother. "Oh, I am fine. I missed

---

[1] Aya – a slang word for mother. It is often added to the names of elderly women

you," she said. In fact, only God knew why she was crying. After greetings, Risolatkhon made tea and came to her brother. "You don't even come to know how your sister lives." "Sister, you know, I am a father of many children, my children are still young, everything will be fine when they grow up," he said, sipping the tea from the cup. The brother and sister sat talking to each other for a long time. When he left, Madaminjon put 50 soums in front of his sister. "Sister, use this needs, if everything is fine, I'll visit you more, take care," he said. When he was saying goodbye, Dilbar came through the gate. She saw her uncle and threw herself into his arms, put her head on his shoulder and cried softly. Her uncle got surprised "Dilbar, my daughter, what happened to you? Has anyone offended you?" The question asked by his uncle remained unanswered. But Dilbar felt that she needed to vent her feelings to someone. She couldn't stop herself and cried out "Uncle, please take us away from here, we are in trouble. My father and my brother quarrel every day because of their drunkenness, there is no peace in our house even for a day, and my poor mother does not have a normal life. Even now, my father is coming drunk." Hearing this, Risolat got worried and said "Brother, you go home. I don't want you to quarrel with him. You know what kind of man he is." Madaminjon said goodbye to his sister reluctantly.

Risolatkhon aya was left alone with her daughter.

Then the mother hugged her daughter and said happily "Dilbar, my daughter your uncle gave us money for your school uniform and your bag." Dilbar said "Mom I have school uniforms and aprons from last year, I will wear them this year as well, they are not worn out yet. Let's buy some flour and oil for this money. I will get my notebooks and books with the money I got in the cocoon fctory. I will get a school uniform next year." Of course Dilbar wanted to wear a new school uniform like all his friends. But, no way. They are in a situation like this ... . Dilbar's eyes were filled with tears again while thinking about this. Dilbar who was in her thoughts was brought to her senses by his father's stern voice. "Dad, shall I make you some tea?" The poor girl begged her father so that another quarrel not to arise.

"Daddy, please, don't drink this wine! I am ashamed of my friends. Don't quarrel with mom!" Dilbar didn't realize that these words came out of her heart, and that she spoke out loud. Days passed one after the other. Before long, the new school year started. The joy of boys and girls hurrying to school early in the morning in school uniforms with flowers in their hands was boundless. Among them is Dilbar, but her face is gloomy. He greeted each friend with confidence. "Dilbar, why are you angry? After all, today is the first of September, you should be happy, my friend." said his friend Marifat. "My dear friend, I couldn't get a new uniform, that's why…"

"That's fine, my dear friend. Your uniform looks brand new."

"Really?"

"Yes, my dear, when did I lie to you? Your uniform suits you very well." Dilbar, who was slightly cheered by Marifat's words, started smiling. But Marifat felt sorry for Dilbar. She tried to make it unnoticeable. When the two friends entered the classroom, everyone was busy choosing their desks."Dilbar, let's sit together, I've got a seat," Dilbar's friend Himayat called. The school years are so different. Frivolous and unaffected period of childhood. That day, Dilbar returned home from school in high spirits. She changed her clothes and did the housework. Her mother had said she would have gone to an ekhsan[2] in the neighborhood. "She must have gone there," she thought to herself, and put the kettle on stove. Now, when she was about to have lunch, her brother came in. He was drunk a bit. When she saw this, she felt uneasy. "Brother, have you

---

[2] A gathering with food. Usually as a remembrance of a passed by person. Reciting Quran is usually observed in ekhsans

drunk again? Do not drink, please, think of our mother! Poor mom is totally worn out. On the one hand dad, on the other you. Brother, let our mother live for us." Dilbar couldn't stop crying and burst into tears. At that moment, his brother said, "Okey, I won't drink any more. I will go to work tomorrow". Although this was not news for Dilbar, she was happy with his brother's words. Her feelings brightened. Dilbar woke up early next morning and swept the yard, sprinkled water and made the whole thing shine. She was about to go to school when her brother came out. "Dilbar, I am going to work in a distant city today. Listen to our mother. I will work and come back. When I come, we will get firewood and coal for the winter. You study well." he said.

"Okay," said Dilbar and went to school. Even after three months passed since her brother left away, nothing was heard of him. In the meantime, the cotton picking period ended. With the money Dilbar collected from picking cotton, they bought coal to for the winter. But they were hopeless with the food. Every day, the mother waited for her son. "Even if he is not the best son, what is he doing in a foreign city?" The mother tried not to remember her child's bad habits. She prayed day and night to God for his health and well-being. They somehow spent that year's horrendous winter. Spring came, and work began in the field. Dilbar went to school until noon, and in the afternoon she went out to work in the field.It was the end of May and soon it was time to go on vacation. The two cherry trees in their garden produced a lot of fruit. Dilbar said to her mother "Mom, shall I pick a couple of buckets of cherries in the morning and take them to the market? We could use the money for household." Risolat Aya said "Okay," and added, "Won't you have trouble picking them, they are too high?" "I can coup with it, I will do it. There is nothing left to boil the pot with.[3] - Dilbar said this and took a bucket. In the evening, Dilbar, who had finished picking two buckets of cherries, turned to his mother and said "Today we will have a meal somehow. God willing, we will have a good shopping tomorrow." Dilbar tried to cheer up her mother. Early in the morning, she took the two buckets of cherries to the market. It seems because of Sunday there were a lot of people in the market. Dilbar sold her buckets of cherries in no time. She seemed to have made a lot of money. At first she wanted to get a little bit of food, but then she thought, "I will take it to my mom first, have a discussion. I don't want to disappoint her." She then left the market and walked towards the house. Since their house was not far away from the market, Dilbar, who soon was at home, saw her mother sitting sadly

---

[3] An Uzbek saying meaning there is no food at home

on the edge of the suri[4], and asked with concern "Are you okay? Why are you sitting quietly like this?" Risolat cried out as soon as she saw Dilbar. "Your brother, has been put in jail there." When Dilbar heard this, it was as if someone poured cold water over her head. "Oh my God! What a grief on our heads? How can I comfort my mother now? What will I do if she gets sick this way?" Even though she was suffering from inside, she didn't ask her mother, "Why?" Now she has to take care of her mother no matter what is going to happen.Difficult days began again for Dilbar. On the one hand, she was worried about her brother, on the other hand, her father's health was not good. Not knowing what to do, Dilbar worked tirelessly in the field.As June drew to a close, the days began to get very hot. Dilbar worked tirelessly. Her friends rested in the coolness of the mulberries on their heads during lunch but Dilbar hilled up beds on the field with her hoe. She envied her friends and wept bitterly over her fate. One such day, Dilbar had a nosebleed. But she hid this situation from her mother. Her nose started bleeding twice almost every day. Even so, she did not want to stay out of the field for even a day. She gradually got exhausted. One day, when the sun was shining hot, she became

---

[4] A large bedlike device made of wood used to sit on, to have meals and sleep, usually for entire family

dizzy and fell in the garden. Seeing this, her friends grabbed Dilbar and took her to the field shed. An ambulance was called from this place. Even when they brought her to the hospital, Dilbar was still unconscious. The bleeding from her nose had not stopped yet. Although the doctors tried their best, Dilbar still did not regain consciousness. The poor mother was running to and fro, even though she begged the doctors to see her daughter, they did not let her in. Dilbar came to her senses when it started to get dark. She couldn't even open her eyes, the head doctor Bakhtiyar, who was stroking the girl's head, suddenly had tears in her eyes: "My daughter, are you alright?" Don't you have pain anywhere? At this time, Dilbar was speechless. It was as if these words were heard from distance. Dilbar, unable to move, lay in this condition for two days. On the third day of her stay in the hospital, she was examined again. According to the results of the examination, Dilbar was diagnosed with typhoid fever. The same day, she was admitted to the department of infectious diseases. However, despite this, the situation got worse. Her high temperature persisted, and her nose went bleeding. Confused, Risolat did not know what to do, she seemed to be numb. At noon, Dilbar lost consciousness. There was not a word left that the mother of the poor girl did not hear from the doctors. Especially the chief doctor spoke harshly to the mother "Why have you made the young girl work so much? The sun hit and even hit from inside! What kind of mother are you? Do you have compassion?" How could they know that Risolat aya had been completely destroyed with her pain?Time passed, and Dilbar's condition began to worsen. She was still unconscious, in the words of the doctors, she was in a "coma". In the meantime, the relatives gathered. Poor mother was heartbroken. Even Dilbar's diseased father arrived. When the doctors said "If three days pass without problems, there is hope that she will be fine." The mother prayed and begged God to heal her daughter continously. It was God's kindness, or mother's prayers were answered whatever it is, on the third day, in the afternoon, Dilbar began to regain consciousness. To the doctor's question "My daughter, are you okay?", Dilbar closed her eyes and gestured "yes," and a tear drop rolled down her face. Seeing this, the doctor said "Don't cry, my daughter. Everything is over," he consoled. But only God and she herself knew what was going through Dilbar's heart and why she was crying. The first word she said was "Song". Because, in her imagination, he remembered the person who sang that song. Then: - How is my mother? Dilbar, who was not able to speak yet, started crying. Seeing this, the nurse asked: - Why are you crying? You are getting better now. Think of your mother. It's been five days. Don't cry. Be happy. You are fine. Everything is over. Dilbar was very comforted by the nurse's words.

The next morning, Dilbar, who was examined by a doctor, was transferred from a special room to a ward. Her condition improved day by day. Since there were infectious patients in the hospital ward where she was being treated, it was not possible to go in or out. Those who came to see the patients would only speak to them through the window. Dilbar felt much better that day. Was it the same dream Dilbar saw from the window of the room, staring at the yellow ripe apricots in the yard, or it is in her mind, she did not know for sure. No, it wasn't a dream, it wasn't a fantasy. When she was in that coma, she remembered some events that happened before her eyes. Dilbar was standing in front of a big mountain. A man with a white beard came out of the mountain cave and patted Dilbar on the head "You will be fine. Have you ever seen a man singing like that? Those guy's songs will be a cure for you. Then Dilbar looked and that singer was singing a song very beautifully. As the singer was among a crowd Dilbar could not see him clearly. But his soft and juicy voice was clearly heard. When Dilbar looked around, the old man was not there anymore. And the song seemed to be coming from closer and closer, louder and louder. Dilbar remembered now that she had come to her senses because of the singer's juicy and soulful voice. At that time, the song was being sang in the courtyard of the hospital. Because of this song that she heard, Dilbar strongly believed "I have returned to life." In fact, it seems to be the case.

The days passed slowly. In the meantime, Dilbar had also recovered a lot. They gave permission to leave the hospital after thirty-seven days. When coming home, Dilbar, who had calmed down a bit, listened to the singer's songs on the radio.

Since then, she wanted to hear those songs every day. Later, when he couldn't hear, he seemed to have lost something. The song seemed to become Dilbar's life. Dilbar was no longer able to work in the fields, so she did not know what to do and thought to herself, "It would be better if I could find some easier work." Suddenly, Marifat opa[5], who lived by the river and sewed hats, came to her mind. "I will learn to sew doppis[6] from her," she thought. She waited for the day to cool down, and in the evening when it was cooler, she asked her mother's to let her go to Marifat's house. Fortunately, Marifat opa was at home. Dilbar

---

[5] Opa- a word added to female names denoting the women is older than the speaker (elder sister)
[6] Doppi – national skullcap

told her everything and asked her to give her some doppis for sewing. Then Marifat opa said.

"You will have to come to my place in order to learn making doppis. It's easier to sew the ornaments for you." She took out five or six workpieces saying that Dilbar would learn quite soon.

"Well, this is for you to learned for now. If sew well, I will pay you fifty tiyins for each piece," she said. When Dilbar came home she was happy that she had find a job. Her mother was cooking dinner over the stove. Dilbar came and sat next to her father who was sitting on the so'ri. "Dad, look, I found a job for myself. Now I will sew doppis." She was joyful like small child. Hearing this, Risolat aya was also happy. When Dilbar was in severe pain, the mother of the poor girl was very much heartbroken. Her father also came to his senses. Since the White Mosque was near his house, he began to attend prayers. It was very quiet at home. But they were worried about the condition of his brother who was far away from them. One day the postman brought a letter which was from Dilbar's brother. The letter was first read by Dilbar herself. There were the following words written. "Hello, my dear ones. How are you? How are you, dear sister? Hasn't the worry of livelihood bent your young body? Are mom and dad ok? Can you forgive your silly brother?

Instead of being with you and taking care of the household, I was fooling around in foreign countries. Here is the result. I'm in a place where I can't get out from. Dilbar, you are a smart girl. Take good care of our father and mother. If I am lucky, I will shoulder all the burden, sister. Say my longing greetings to my father and mother. Goodbye until I see you again by mail. I look forward to your reply to my letter." Dilbar immediately replied to the letter. In her letter, she wrote that they were healthy, that they were living peacefully, and in short, everything was good. She did not write that she had been sick or the difficulties she had experienced. She did not want to him embarrassed and at the end of the letter added "Brother, take care of yourself. Don't worry about us," and finished the letter. The mother's heart brightened a lot when she found out that the letter came from her son. She stood there with tears in his eyes. Days followed days and the new academic year began. In the meantime, Dilbar's uncle came and brought her some school clothes, textbooks and notebooks and a bag. He left the money again. Risolat aya was happy and said "God bless my brother. He's doing a lot for us. He got over his own children and bought clothes for you." Days passed one after the other.It was the middle of September, that day everyone went out to pick cotton. Because it Dilbar was not good enough to pick cotton, they gave him a discharge from the hospital. At the beginning of December, all students and teachers returned to school. One day when Dilbar came to class, her friend Muyassar was sitting at her desk. Dilbar said calmly "Hey my frienf, this place was mine. Let me take my seat." "No, I won't. You go and take the last desk. Don't join us from today because you've had typhoid fewer. Don't spread it about! And you are also poor. This is not your place. Know your place!" She pushed Dilbar. Humiliated, Dilbar left the classroom with her bag. Her classmates went out to the schoolyard after her and said "Come back, Dilbar." But Dilbar could not bear these insults and cried out. By the time Dilbar came home, her eyes were swollen with tears. Risolat Aya asked "What happened, my dear daughter?

"I just have a headache." At that time, Dilbar was studying in eighth grade. "I won't go to school anymore, I'll find a job and work."

It is better to work and support my parents than to study in such a difficult situation. How long will we be dependent on my uncle? How long will I hear from my classmates such insulting words? I have had enough. I will work!" Dilbar made such a decision and got up and went to her neighbor Motabar's opa. "Opa, do you have any work?" Dilbar cried. Then she told her what happened. "I will go and ask today. I'll tell you if it's all right. You can also go to school with me in the evening school. There is also an eighth grade in the evening school. Don't be upset. "Thank you, opa, please help me," said Dilbar, who was slightly cheered by Motabar's words. It turned out that Mo'tabar opa did not tell lies. She took Dilbar with her the next day. Dilbar recognized the master opa as soon as she saw her. It was Umida opa from that cocoon factory. "What will we do with your school? Do you hear me?""No, I want to study at evening school. That day, Umida opa put Dilbar to wash the empty bread forms. It seems that the master liked the work of Dilbar, who washed the forms very much cleanly, so said "Come tomorrow too," gave two loaves of bread and added while saying goodbye "Take them home."Dilbar said "Thank you, opa, for hiring me. I will not forget your kindness." When Dilbar entered the house, Risolat aya had made hot tea on the stove. Dilbar set the table and placed the soft bred she had just brought on the table. Father and mother were drinking tea. Dilbar, for some reason, seemed to be satisfied with what she had done. When she told her mother over tea that she was going to evening school, both his father and mother did not agree at first. Dilbar explained the situation slowly and persuaded them. There are many students in the evening school.Dilbar went to the director. He explained the situation clearly

"Teacher, please accept me to the evening school. I've also convinced my parents that I would continue studying at the evening school. I want to work and study. Please, teacher, don't say no. I promise not to drop out my study. So Dilbar started working during the day and studying at evening school.

Five days later, the class leader came to Dilbar's house. The homeroom teacher, who knew all about the situation, reported everything to the principal. The principal, getting to know the situation, first scolded the homeroom teacher. Then he ordered to call Dilbar with her mother in the morning. Dilbar, who returned home late in the evening, was speechless when she heard everything from her mother. "No, I won't study. I will work! I just can't stop working. Mom, if it's winter, we need firewood and coal. Don't worry, I will go to the school in the morning and tell the principal. I am now employed. I will also study. When she was about to go to work in the morning, someone called the house. Looking out Dilbar saw Abdukarim Oktamov, the homeroom teacher. "Assalomy alaykum."

After greeting? the teacher the appointed Dilbar to go to school. When Dilbar entered the school with her mother, the headmaster was discussing something with a couple of teachers in the corridor. As soon as he saw Dilbar, he walked towards his room. The director and three or four teachers gathered in the room. "What is it, my girl? Why aren't you coming to school?" Dilbar tried to answer slowly, but tears filled her eyes and she struggled to speak. "Domla[7], you know, I am a single girl." My parents are very old. They don't work. My father receives an allowance of twelve soums. What can we buy for that? How will we live if I don't work? Please teacher, I have just got a job. Do not let me lose my job. I will continue my studies in evening school. The director listened to Dilbar's words and said, "My daughter, you are still young. You better study. These difficult days will pass. Come, I will give you a job at this school. Only in the name of your mother. And you will continue to do the work, you will work as a cleaner. After the classes, you can easily catch up. Agreed? Now, go to class and continue your lessons. It will also help your mother to retire. Is it okay, my daughter? The director said so kindly that Dilbar couldn't say no. After leaving the director's room, Dilbar went straight to the bakery.

Is Umida opa waiting for her? As soon as Umida opa saw Dilbar she asked, "Why are you late today, my daughter? It's almost ten o'clock? Dilbar told Umida everything and apologized to her. "Opa, thank you for

---

[7] Domla – male teacher (usually respected senior teacher)

everything." she said. As she was leaving, Umida called Dilbar to her side. She gave four soft loafs of bread and ten soums in her hand and said, "If you want, come and work in the second shift. I hope this will help you, my daughter." She also appointed.

"I will try, opa. Thank you again." Dilbar came home happily. She gave the money to her mother and made tea herself. Risolat aya said. "You drink tea with your father, my daughter. I will go to the market and buy some things." For some reason, Dilbar was very happy today. There are good people too. As it was winter, a light snow started to fall when Dilbar went out into the yard. Dilbar took the firewood left in the open to a more sheltered place and said to herself, "there are little firewood and coal. Will it be enough? At the worst, we will cut one of the large branches of the apricot tree. We must also leave some brunches to blossom in the spring?" she said when she entered the house. Risolt was cooking soup on the stove. "Mother, there is small firewood. This year the winter is going to be harsh I think"

"Yes, my daughter, there is little wood left. I saw your Ibrahim aka[8] the other day. He said he would bring some firewood. No wonder he

---

[8] Aka- elder brother, a word added to male names denoting the man is older than the speaker ()

brings it. Don't think too much about everything. Take care of your health, my dear daughter. God gave you back to me, my sweety." Dilbar became sad a little again. Those days, the song she had heard, the old man all of them began to flash in her mind. "Why did this happen? Was it a dream or a real event?" Dilbar still couldn't get over it. "Even if it was a dream, why did it appear to me? No matter what happened, that old man did not enter my dreams for nothing." Dilbar could not think. She picked up a book to distract herself, but it didn't work. Her mind was confused. Her father's words still stuck in her mind. In the morning, Dilbar did not want to go to school, and went to the market. As soon as she entered the class, his friends surrounded her, "You did well, Dilbar, came back to school. We will study together." Dilbar said "Thank you," and went to the last desk and sat down. The first lesson was chemistry. Anvarhon Madumarova entered the classroom and immediately said, "Dilbar, stand up." Dilbar looked at the teacher with frightened eyes. "Children do you all know Dilbar?" the teacher asked. The children were a bit surprised by this unexpected question but said, "Yes, we know her, we know her."

"No, you don't know her, if you had known her, you wouldn't have showmen such disrespect. This a girl who is sacrificing herself for the wellbeing of her old parents, though she is still a little girl. You know him now. While you were busy having fun, this poor girl was looking for a job to earn a living for her loved ones. She worked wholeheartedly at the bread factory. And now, starting from today, she helps her mother by washing the floor in our school and also studies. From now on, if any of you mock or laugh at Dilbar, you will not hear a good thing from me! Dilbar, sit down my daughter. Blessings! At this age, you are running for a living, thinking of your parents and doing a good job. These days will pass. God willing, you will get into good studies. It's like you haven't seen it yet. I am proud of you." From the teacher's words, Dilbar couldn't control herself and cried while laying her head on the desk. Dilbar didn't talk to anyone until the end of classes that day. When the bell rang to end the last class, Dilbar left the classroom before everyone else. So Dilbar started studying at school and cleaning after school hours. At first it was a little difficult, but after three or four days she got used to it. Although her mother said, "I will go out and help." Dilbar said, "I will do it myself. You will suffer in the cold." May be Allah had mercy on this family, winter did not last long, and the spring season came earlier. It started raining. At such times, it was really difficult to control the elementary school pupils. They would run into the classrooms with muddy feet and Dilbar would stay at the door.

When it was Risolat aya's shift, Dilbar was always there to help her.

Days passed one after the other quickly. Little by little, their lives also changed. There was flour and oil in bags at home. Dilbar would be happy about that. It was May then. One day, classmates wanted to climb Chilustin mountain. Dilbar's friend Makhfirat said, "Dilbar, will you go out too? Only girls will go together. If you go, we will pick tulips." Dilbar wanted to go, but was hesitating, thinking that even if it was a day off, there was much household work and her mother could have some difficulties. Noticing this, Soliykha asked, "After all, it is Sunday tomorrow, a day off? You don't have work. Comon, come with us."

"Okay, let's see," replied Dilbar. When they were eating in the evening, Dilbar asked her mother, "My friends are going hiking in the mountains tomorrow, may I also go?"

"What about you, my sweet girl?" Risolat aya asked her daughter who was sitting thoughtfully.

"I don't know."

"Why don't you know? You also go. You will have some walk. You are tired. You will have a little rest at least" said the mother. Dilbar said, "OK" to hermother's words, and began to clean the table and dishes.

The mountain air is always pleasant. Every year, it is customary for the residents of the district to celebrate the first day of May in this garden. It has a very large area, and in this garden there are a lot of cherry trees; it is very cool and a people forget all their problems. That's probably why, every spring, a lot of people come to these places. The girls spoke to each other without stopping and did not even noticed that they had arrived. First of all, everyone put on the dastarhan[9] everything they had brought from home. After having some things to eat, they went to the mountain.

"Who wants to go up," Mukarram Khon said. Because the tulips grew in higher places. Dilbar barely climbed to the top of the mountain. She felt tired for some reason. "I will stay here," she said, and sat down on a rock. From where she was sitting, the distant places could clearly be seen. As she was looking into the distance, a certain feeling of warmth rushed to her chest. Joy flashed in her eyes. How beautiful life is when looking at the distance! Just then, some divine words began to come to her mind. Unfortunately, she did not have a pen or any piece of paper with her. She vividly remembered the words that came to her mind. At that moment, a bird landed on a mountain rock nearby. Remembering this situation, Dilbar

---

[9] A special table cloth that can be laid on the ground

found such words that she could not help but admit to these divine words, "Where are these words coming to me from?" Dilbar came home and wrote down the lines she remembered. Gradually, her interest in poetry began to increase. One day, while listening to the singer's songs, her passion for him, the fame she was finding, her verses written with affection, her beautiful love, her dreams, turned into beautiful lines. How miraculous were those words, the bird perched on that mountain rock, the villages visible from afar, were a page for the poem being written. Dilbar slowly began to find words out of nowhere.

She found words that were all for the singer whose song brought Dilbar back to life. Two years later, those words turned into a beautiful poem. But Dilbar was not expecting such a beautiful poem, so she felt happy in the very heart. Dilbar was now in the tenth grade when this poem found its place in the world of poetry. One day, Dilbar, who read an article by a poet from Osh Ganijon Kholmatov *About relation to Poetry* in the newspaper "Lenin Yoli" (Lenin's way) published in Osh at that time, went to Osh in search of the domla. She met him and showed him the poem she had written. Then Ganijon Kholmatov corrected some shortcomings of the poem, removed one line, and then wished Dilbar a safe journey. That was the first poem Dilbar wrote. At that time, when the master poet Ganijon Kholmatov (Mughanniy) said to Dilbar, "Come, girl, let's give this poem of yours to a good artist (singer)." Dilbar believed and said, "Domla, I wrote this poem for a person, I can't give it to anyone." After that event Dilbar fell in love with writing poetry. However, no matter how much she wrote, she could not compare them to that first poem. One day there was an event at school. There Dilbar read the poem she wrote for the first time on the school stage. After that she began to participate in school and district events with her poems. Later, Dilbar's poems began to be published in the newspaper "Lenin Yoli" published in Osh and in the newspapers "Lenin Uchkuni" (Lenin's Spark) from the Uzbek publishing house. Meanwhile, Dilbar, who was about to complet her tenth grade, preferred to work rather than study. "Because," she said "what will happen to my parents if I go to study?"

After graduating from school and passing her final exams, Dilbar was transferred to a spinning and weaving factory in Osh, where she started working. A bus would pick her up in the morning and drop her off in the evening. The double-shift work suited Dilbar. Her classmates started studying in different places. Those who couldn't go to institute got a job at the factory where Dilbar was working. Once, at the end of the day, Dilbar said to his mother, "Now you also have some rest, mother, don't work at the school as a cleaner." Risolat aya said, "You don't say so, my girl, I'm not getting tired. She didn't get tired of saying, "It'll be at least a little help to you." Dilbar would help her mother on the days when she worked at the second shift. A month later, when Dilbar, who received her monthly salary, came home, a lot of firewood and cotton tree were thrown in front of the gate. Entering the house, Dilbar was relieved when she heard from her mother that her aunt's son had come. While giving the salary to her mother she said, "Mother, let's buy the coal tomorrow, we will take care of the rest" Days passed one after the other. Spring came quite soon. In her spare time, Dilbar took up to poetry again. It was the first months of summer when Dilbar came home from work and saw that the wall separating their house from the street had collapsed. When Risolat saw Dilbar, who did not know what to do, she said "Look, my dear daughter, now we have this onto our heads."

"Okay, mother. Don't worry about it. We will find a way through this," she scolded said to her mother. But to herself, "What are we going to do now? Whom shall we ask for help?" Because it was a summer time, days were long. Dilbar began to separate and restore the fallen guvalaks[10]. By the time the day was

---

[10] Guvalak – a special mud bricks of oval shape

approaching it's end, she had cleaned less than half of it.

When Risolat Aya said "Come, my daughter, it's late now, stop it," Dilbar said, "Okey," and started washing her face and hands. On her way to the kitchen, she gently said to her mother who was cooking, "Tomorrow is Sunday, tomorrow we will make clay and erect the wall from anew. It can't remain open like this. It looks ugly from the street." Dilbarni could not go to sleep for a long time. She read through her notebook where she had been writing her poems.

"I have written a lot of poems," she said, smiling to herself as she jotted down the verses that came to her mind. In the morning, Dilbar got up at dawn, first she gathered the guvalaks, and then started to make the clay. It suddenly sounded like as if someone was calling. Then she saw that her classmate Hosilbek was looking at her. He said hurriedly "We are coming to help."

"What kind of help? Who said it to you?" Dilbar, who was embarrassed, looked at Khosilbek while cleaning the mud from her hands. "Now, the guys will also come. We don't have anything today. Let's have a khashar[11] today. You cook a

---

[11] Khashar – some people working together for free as a help for the owner of the house

pilaf, leave the wall to us. Soon the guys will also come. Dilbar hastily washed her face and hands and made some tea.

Soon, other classmates also arrived. They told each other jokes and started the work. Dilbar was happy to have such classmates. Seven or eight guys completed the wall in the afternoon. They praised the meal prepared by Dilbar. When leaving, Dilbar gave each of them a kerchief she had woven herself, "Thank you! You helped me on my difficult day. How could I have built this wall without you? Thanks to everyone, stay healthy," she said with tears in her eyes. "Dilbar, don't hesitate to us if you have any difficulty," said her classmates. Dilbar, saw them out and returned, came and sat next to her father, "Dad, our wall is now strong," she said with a smile.

"Let them find blessings," said Risolat aya, who was doing something at the stove. Her father prayed for a long time. Dilbar, who had eaten a little, went to clean the rest of the guwalak soil. - Hey girl, relax. Are you home tomorrow? You will do it tomorrow. - said his mother. - Is it worth it? It's still early, I'll be right away - said Dilbar, while spreading the soil with a hoe.

At that moment, uncle Kadir came in. "Come, uncle," greeted Dilbar without hesitation. - Why did he come? Dilbar thought. He didn't like his uncle very much because he didn't get any news during his difficult days. There was another reason. Dilbar did not even go to school at that time. One day the police came and searched their house. Dilbar, who was not aware of anything, wondered what was going on. The grass that grew on one side of their yard, which looked like some kind of grass, was mowed somewhere for inspection. Due to this incident, Dilbar's father was imprisoned for two years. Then his uncle came and beat Dilbar with his mother. At that time, his uncle pushed Dilbar and his brother, who cried, "Don't insult my mother!" Dilbar hated his uncle because of this incident. It was not in vain that Dilbar was impressed. At one time, he left the house where his father and uncle lived after quarreling. This father's house is named after the charmer's father. Now, years later, he wanted to get information from his brother in order to transfer this house to his name. When he told his brother about this over tea, he listened calmly.

After that, he slowly began to speak, "You know how many difficult days I have seen. I am quite an old man now. No matter how many difficulties I had, I have not fought for the house. Whatever happened, I dug up mud and built this house together with your sister-in-law, my wife. What did you do to help as my brother? Or did I ask for help? I won't ask for any. You can transfer the house to your name," he said, putting down the cup upside down. Not knowing what to do, his brother was going to leave when Risolat aya stopped him saying the dinner was ready and made him sit down and she herself went to the stove. Even in his difficult days when he was alcohol addict didn't Dilbar's father need other people's things. And now, when he reached a certain age, he did not want to hurt his brother's feeling either. "It's okay, he is my brother, he has got his children, don't worry. May he not see the days I saw. I have one foot in the grave, he will realize his guilt?" he said to Risolat aya. Dilbar was openly happy for these words of his father's.

Days passed one after the other. One day, a distant relative came to see them and told that his neighbor's son was in prison with Tursunboy. That a letter had arrived the day before where the guy said, "We will both be going out of prison in the next few days." Risolat Aya, who was happy about this, said, "May he come home safely" with tears in her eyes. In fact, they had come to woo Dilbar under this pretext.

Aunt Ma'mura, not knowing what to say, began to speak slowly, "I know your daughter is still young, but isn't it better to let her merry if there is a suitable couple for her?" You have a discussion." Risolat aya having seen off the guests, entered the house following the guests.

Her head was buzzing. It was noisy as if a bee was flying there.

"What should I do now? The suitors who came today made her think that her daughter is still young. Looking carefully at Dilbar, the mother noticed that her daughter had grown into a beautiful young maiden. "May God grant you happiness," Risolat said with tears in her eyes. But she did not tell his daughter that they were suitors. "What do I do, in a hurry? Let her brother come, if he works honestly, if he helps with the dowry, then we will see," she thought. One by one, Dilbar's friends working at the factory began to prepare documents for submission to study. Dilbar, who was envious of them, said, "I wish I could go with them to study." But she knew it was impossible. Even so, she said, "It is a dream," and continued her work.

One day, when Dilbar came home from work, a little girl was playing in the yard. There were blankets and household things everywhere. "What is this? What is going on?" said Dilbar worriedly. "Nothing special, the house on the other side is empty. They need a place to live. Let them stay in that house. I couldn't say no when they asked. We will play with the child too, my daughter. She had become already become like her own granddaughter. Dilbar went out after having some tea and helped the neighbor woman. This way she got acquainted with her new neighbors.

It was great to have new neighbors for Dilbars. Dilbar, who went to work early in the morning, sometimes did not even have time to sweep the yard. The woman next door was also kind and polite. In a couple of days, she and Dilbar became like sisters. One day, the neighbor woman, who was waiting for Dilbar to come home from work, called her to the house where she was living.

"What is it, sister?" Dilbar said. I haven't even changed my clothes yet.

"Everything is fine. I only wanted to cook pilaf together with you today. We'd sit together and talk. I've liked you like my own younger sister. What do you say?" "Well, I'll change my clothes and prepare things for the pilaf."

"No need, I've already prepared everything. All you have to do is to stay by my side."

"Okay sister," said Dilbar proudly. "I wish I had a sister like her." Dilbar dreamed of it. It seems that the woman next door also went through a lot of difficulties. When she was ten years old, she became an orphan after her mother and was brought up by her aunt with difficulty. Moreover, her father, got married a second time, had another children and stopped paying attention to his elder daughter.

"Not long after my mother passed, my father got married. For some reason, my stepmother did not like me. They gave me away to my aunt. I looked after my aunt's children, and I could barely finish the eighth grade without going to school sometimes. My aunt used to say that there was little good of girls' studying, so did not even send me to study. I was busy taking care of my aunt's children. One day, my aunt's husband (my pochcha[12]) came home drunk and beat my aunt. I heard the words, "Get rid of that orphan. Hearing those words, something inside me seemed to break. I did not know where to throw myself, where to go. I couldn't stop the tears from my eyes. When I thought about it, I realized that it was not easy for aunt too. There were few words left that her husband did not say about me. If not every day, then there were fights every other day. One day, two women came to my aunt's house. My and Aunt and her husband talked to them for a long time. Then they looked at me and the elderly woman said, "She is a very beautiful girl."

I stood there not understanding anything. My aunt, who came back after she saw the guests off said, "Come with me into the house, I have something to say." My pochcha coughed and said, "I must water the sheep," and went away. I followed my aunt into the house without

---

[12] Pochcha – elderly sister's or aunts husband

understanding anything.

"Lola, you are eighteen. Now it's time for you to get married. Think of me too. The women who have come were suitors. They came to ask for you. The fellow is a brother of your pochcha's close friend. They say it is a good family. If you meet the boy tomorrow, then we will give permission." Seeing my aunt's condition, I had no choice but to say, "Okay." The next day I went to the place that my aunt told me. To be honest, I didn't like the guy's behavior and words. He looked very arrogant and spoke of grandiloquent things, it felt like I was being ignored.

After that, my life became a mess. They wanted to kick me out of their house because I didn't marry the boy they had found. I had no place to go, thinking that I would not be able to fit my father in his house, so I had to adapt. The wedding took place very hurriedly. What would a wedding be like without mom? After the wedding, I lived well for about a month. I don't even want to remember my life after that." Lola opa sighed, "We will talk about the rest tomorrow. I made you tired you too. You have to go to work tomorrow morning," she said. Wishing her a good night, Dilbar also went in their own house. But Lola opa's words did not leave her imagination. She could not go to sleep for quite a bit.

Dilbar's thoughts reminded her of those difficulties. 1966, after the Tashkent earthquake, everyone was in panic. Dilbar's father was in prison at that time. Her brother worked as an assistant in a teahouse by the river. He would not come home even at night. Dilbar, who was left alone with his mother, stayed awake until morning because of fear.

It looked scary at night because of the large yard walls. At that time, neither her uncle nor her aunt would ever visit them. One of those days, Risolat Aya took Dilbar to her to her aunt's.

"It had been eight months since your brother got jailed. I havn't come to ask you for anything. We are handling things ourselves. There is only one request. Please help just once. Help us visit your brother. I can't do it alone. Please help a little." Poor Risolat could not continue as was interrupted by her sister-in-law. Dilbar's aunt was so much rude to her that even Dilbar began to cry when she saw her mother crying.

"What? Do you think I am a rich woman for you? Or my brother, did he leave me a treasure? Are you asking me for money? Go away, I don't want even to see you. Get your small fry out of here. Don't come back again. Her aunt insulted them so much that Risolat couldn't stand it anymore and left her sister-in-law with Dilbar. A child is a child. Dilbar was hungry when they left her aunt's house.

"Mom, I want to eat," she said to her mother. Unaware that this would have happen, the mother said, "Now we will have something to eat at your uncle's. We will soon be there." Remembering this on the way, the mother was heartbroken. She was also embarrassed in front of his daughter. When they came home, it was not yet noon.

Risolat Aya had finished a pair of *bird deer chorsi*[13] given to her by a neighbor. In this situation she went to her neighbor, "Munnavarkhon, I have finished the chorsis. That's why... I'm going to my brother's, she said, trying to hide her red eyes from crying. Munavvar Khon seemed to feel this, "Is everything OK? Why are you crying?" Risolat was full of tears, so burst into tears. She told the whole story while crying. What have you gone to her? You know what kind of person she is? Why didn't you come up to me? If you had asked me, wouldn't I give it to you?" Her neighbor felt sorry for Risolat. That's why she used to give money for the service of making a bird and deer chorsi, saying, "If I gave money, she wouldn't receive it." This is why she would

---

[13] Chorsi – special traditional belt made of different type of fabric (mainly silk).
   Bird dear chorsi – special (expensive) type of chorsi

give her chorsis to be sewn and pay for them.

Risolat left her house with the money given for a couple of chorsis. Trying to ease herself started to clean the house. But it didn't help. Her sister-in-law's words kept ringing in her mind. She was ready to cry out any time and finally did it. "It's hard for me to wait until the dawn," she said, started to get ready to set off. Dilbar was happy when she heard that they were going to her uncle's[14] house. It is good there, she has a friend Odinakhon, they play together. A good uncle does not scold her like her aunt. Risolat arrived at his father's house with Dilbar in the evening.

Her brother and his children were eating in the open air. As soon as the children saw their aunt, they shouted, "Our aunt has come." Seeing that they were happy, Risolat aya got happy too. They talked for a long time with her brother's wife Zulfiyakhon around the table. The children were arguing one by one, "I'll sleep with my aunt." "No, I will sleep with her." Only Dilbar was sitting on the side watching them.

Risolat's father, Ortiqboy, had passed away not long ago. She went to the cemetery with her sister-in-law Zulfiyakhon. She cried there with her bitter tears. Thinking about those events, Dilbar had tears in her eyes. "As far back as I

---

[14] Mother's brother

can remember, I have always been a witness to my poor mother's sufferings. Being a mother or a woman, like many, she did not live comfortably." Her neighbor Lolakhon also had a hard time from the beginning. She got divorced when her daughter was one-year-old. When her aunt (mother's sister) did not let her home, she wandered in different places. Desperate, Lola went to her aunt (father's sister). When her aunt found out about what happened, she took Lola and her child to house of Dilbar's father and persuaded her to live in her mother's house. But soon, Lola, who could not even fit in her father's house, began to face life's difficulties again. After some time, with someone's help, she came to Dilbars' house. One day Lola asked Dilbar a question.

"Why haven't you studied?"

"No, it's not just about studying. I don't try to study myself. I cannot leave my parents alone. There is no one to look after them. If my brother comes, I will be able to study," said Dilbar sadly.

"Dilbar, my sister, you must study at university. Trust me. You will see, you will go to study. If you are lucky, you will definitely become a student."

"Thank you," said Dilbar in disbelief. Was it Lolakhon's speech or something else but Dilbar, who was not interested in studying before, now started thinking about it. She was thinking about it all day at work too. "What will people say if I get lucky enough to study at university? Won't people say that I have left my old parents and gone to some city to study. How can she dare to study? What if people start to gossip? No, I won't go. It was okay if my brother was here." Dilbar was talking to herself and didn't even notice that her working time was over.

Seeing Dilbar, who entered the house in a sad mood, Risolat aya said, "My dear daughter, do you have any pain?", she was worried.

"No, I'm fine, I'm tired a bit," Dilbar said, and went into the house. After dinner, Dilbar told her mother about studying. In fact, her mother was very happy, "It is a good idea of yours, my daughter."

"I was going to apply, but... you and dad are alone at home."

"You are my nutty kid. These days will pass away. Your brother will come soon. Lolakhon is looking after us. Don't worry." She tried to cheer up her daughter.

When she said to her father, he said, "Study well, my daughter, if we are here today, we will be gone tomorrow." He said. "Try hard, learn and you will be successful."

Dilbar thought about his father's words again. "What if they get sick without me? Who will look after them. No, I will not leave them." While she was thinking like this, Lolakhon opa called her up. After saying hello, Dilbar said, "Opa, I want to apply to university. But I hesitate thinking about my father and mother. It would be a different story if my brother was here. What will happen to them if I leave? Both mom and dad agreed."

"Then go. Don't worry. I'll take care of them until your brother comes. I treat them as my parents. After all, I also need some sawab. Besides, they have given me a shelter. I will take my daughter to kindergarten and will work. Feel free to study. Then you will be grateful to me."

"Thank you, sister, God sent you to me. I will not forget your kindness." Tears filled Dilbar's eyes. But she tried to hide her tears. So Dilbar began to prepare her documents to apply. Three or four days before she left for Tashkent, his aunt (father's siter) suddenly came in. She was nervous and angry up to the sky and shouted. "How can you dare to go to study? When your father is alive, let him see your wedding party. You cannot study, you are poor. My brother could not have pleasure out of you two. One is only bringing problems. And now this one. If I don't correct the situation, you can go to the city and get married to someone. You are Machiavellian! You won't go to study. Look at your father's condition." Dilbar could not stand his aunt's insulting words. Risolat aya, who did not know what to do, said, "Sister, let her study and walk among her peers, she is spending her youth in hard work. He hasn't gone anywhere and hasn't played and hasn't had fun. Let her go. If she gets enrolled, it is good, if she doesn't she will come back and go on working."

Her aunt got even more angry, "It's all your fault, you're spoiling the child. No! That's it! You won't go! We will say OK to the suitors who came the other day. Let my brother see your wedding while he is still alive."

"What matchmakers?" I don't have any dowry yet. Are you going to marry me? What do we have? Enough! First think then speak. Enough! You've harassed my poor mother so much. What did she mother see in her life? She only saw your vituperation. Do you want me to be like her?" Dilbar cried uncontrollably. Then her angry aunt said, "Well, do what you want! You have brought a widow into your home. Will you still take her as a bride?" she said, looking at Lolakhon. "Brother, I'm leaving," she said and left. Dilbar's father was a bit deaf , and looked at his sister in surprise, not understanding anything. Dilbar looked at his mother as if to say, "Mom, what is this?"

"Okay, my girl, don't pay attention. Later she will recover."

However, Dilbar could not recover. Her aunt's words had had a strong effect on her. "She didn't even poped in, not a single time when we were in trouble. And now she wants to be the boss again?" Dilbar could not stop her tears and went to Lolakhon who was washing clothes.

"Who is that woman?" Dilbar came to herself from his question. "Huh? My aunt" she said, wiping her tears.

"Don't be offended, with her words. You do as I say. Such days have happened to me too." These words of Lolakhon comforted her.

Dilbar said, "Okay, I'm going to study in Tashkent", but she was thinking about how to find her way when in such a big city like Tashkent. She and her friend Khadija found three or four girls who were studying for librarins until their before the dusk, and talked to them. "If you are not in a hurry, I will leave the day after tomorrow. We can go together. You won't even look for it. I will help you apply." Said one of them.

"Okay, I'll wait," said Dilbar, laughing happily and Dreaming of being a student like that girl.

"Agreed. Then I will wait for you at the bus

station at ten o'clock. Don't be late, because there is a long line to get a ticket now."

"Okay," Dilbar said, trying to hide her joy. As soon as she saw her, Holida, who was waiting for Dilbar, said, "Let's go," and walked towards the bus. In fact, it is very difficult to get a ticket. "Is everyone going to study?" Dilbar asked Holida.

"A lot of study, a lot of work," she said, and went to buy a ticket. Holida received two tickets in about an hour. "Our seats are behind the bus. I am thankful for that. There is still a long time for the bus to leave. Let's go into the garden and talk in a cool place. We will half an hour before the bus leaves.

"Okay," said Dilbar and followed Khalida. "It's beautiful, isn't it?" Dilbar, who saw these places for the first time, looked around.

"No," Holida said, "this Asaka is not much, you should see Tashkent." Holida boasted with enthusiasm. When they were sitting in the garden, for some reason, Dilbar wanted to go home. She asked Holida some uestions in order to distract herself. Still, some kind of confusion fell into her heart. "That's how I see it now. What will I do when I am far away? Her thoughts were with her parents.

"As my aunt said, how can I dare to study? Couldn't I work quietly and look at my parents?"

At four o'clock, the bus left the Asaka branch station. Dilbar was looking around because her seat was on the window side, and she was slightly distracted. Time was going by, the bus moved further and further away, and it was getting dark. The lanterns on the distant stilts gave off a dim light.

Holidakhon was three or four years older than Dilbar. Dilbar, who did not want to disturb the sleep of Holida, who was sleeping with her head on the backrest of the seat, began to remember those difficult days again until she was far away. There were a lot of poplar trees in Dilbar's house. When her uncle came to their home, he asked for five or six poplar trees. "Sister, you know that I am building a house. This house will be left to my brother Omonillo. I have to finish the house as soon as possible. Please help, I won't also stand by." Then Risolatkhon, in tears, told her brother what happened the previous night.

"For ten soums, I heard so many things. If I let you cut down the poplars, I will be in trouble again. I'll ask your pochcha first when I get there. He won't say no and I'll let you know," she said calmly. Her brother liked her idea? "I still haven't been able to do anything to commemorate our father." Risolatkhon was upset. "I am poor."

"Don't think about it, sister. When your children grow up, you will forget all about these days. I only wish my pochcha came safely. Don't think about it too much." The brother and sister talked to each other for quite long time.

"Now, brother, I must go home. There is nobody there," said Risolatkhon after breakfast in the morning. "I will come again," Dilbar, who heard that they were leaving, did not want to go. She came up to her mother and beggad, "Let's stay for one more day." However, she had to agree with her mother when the latter said firmly they should leave.

That day, when they came home, there was a lot of water and the yard was flooded. "Just what we need," she said, putting the things in her hands on the so'ri, and ran to the ditch on the edge of the yard to block the water. Dilbar followed her mother and rushed to help through the mud. Due to the large size of the yard, it had been very difficult to water the garden. It is not for nothing that they say *unhappiness is under your feet.* When Risolatkhon was blocking the ditch in front of the house, her foot accidentally slipped and she fell down. She lost consciousness because her head fell with a hard blow on the stone at the edge of the platform. Frightened, Dilbar ran into the street screaming. Her mother's head was bleeding when the neighbors ran in. Neighbors who saw this immediately called an ambulance.

They put Risolat aya on the bed at the so'ri until the ambulance arrived. Dilbar trembled and wiped the blood from his mother's head with her hand, and tears was pouring from her eyes. Poor woman, this was the only thing missing then. Habibakhon opa found a towel somewhere and cried while cleaning the blood that was streaming from her head. "Poor little soul hasn't seen a single happy day," she thought. In the meantime, an ambulance arrived. The courtyard was instantly filled with people. Someone cursed the gardener who opened the water. After the doctor came, Risolatkhon came to herself.

"We must take her to the hospital," said the doctor who was quite a plumb man. "She has had a head injury, and she needs to be X-rayed. Are there any men to help to carry her into the ambulance car?" Unfortunately, there were no men, and a group of women carried the litter to the car.

"I will go together with her," said Habibakhon.

"Dilbar, wash your face, my daughter." Dilbar, who came to her senses from Munavvar aunt's voice, hurriedly came to the edge of the stream. Having washed the blood from her face, she ran after the car that was taking her mother.

"Come back Dilbar, we will go together." She didn't even hear the calls of her neighbors and ran after the car. The car increased its speed after turning onto the highway and vanished from Dilbar's sight. The girl, not knowing what to do, ran to her brother with tears in her eyes. Fortunately, one day, she had visited the tea house where her brother worked with her mother to get news from him. Her brother saw his sister in this situation, "What happened? When did you come?"

"Right now," cried Dilbar. She explained the incident to her brother.

"Go home. I will go to the hospital myself," he said and ran away. Dilbar reluctantly came home because she was afraid of his brother.

Dilbar was sitting alone on the edge of the so'ri in the yard where there was nobody beside herself when it seemed to her as though someone called her. She went to the gate and looked, and when she sat down again, she began to cry. At that moment, she saw some blood on the blanked where her mother had been lying, dragged it to the edge of the ariq.[15] It was too heavy for her to drag for so long, and she poured water in a bowl on it and washed. Dilbar, whose eyes were swollen from crying,

---

[15] Ariq – small stream

sat down in front of the gate. As it was a hot day, there was no one on the street. She looked out to see if her brother was coming and sat down again. Her did not come, he ente brother didn't appear, and she entered the house again. Her mother lying in a pool of blood appeared before her eyes again. She cried and cried. She was crying not because she was alone, but because she was afraid of her mother's condition. "What shall I do? I wish my brother would come."

Her brother wasn't coming as evil. Dilbar, startled at a voice, and looked at the street. "You are my sweet girl; you must be hungry. Come and have something to eat. Don't worry your mom is OK. She will be discharged in two or three days, don't be afraid."

On hearing this, Dilbar who got very cheerful even though she was young.

"Have a good meal. Then we will go to the hospital together." Dilbar was shocked by this word.

"Are we really going?" She immediately washed her face and hands. Of course I will take you."

Habiba opa made Dilbar to have some mastava[16] and took her to the hospital. They did not let her in at the hospital. They gave the

---

[16] Mastava – rice soup

food they brought from another side and went to the rear window. Habibakhon picked up Dilbar and showed her to her mother. The mother's head was tied with gauze. She was lying looking at the ceiling. She could not even look at Dilbar. Seeing her mother, Dilbar did not take her eyes off her while wiping the tears from her eyes. "No matter what happens, may it end well," she said thought childlishly.

Dilbar, who was returning after visiting her mother's, carefully looked at everything on the way, so as not to be mistaken while coming again tomorrow. When they reached the corner, the teahouse where her brother worked could be seen. "My brother is there," said Dilbar, feeling like bursting into teras. Dilbar, for some reason, wanted to see her brother, looked at Habiba opa as if to say, "Let's go in."

"Women are not allowed to enter this tea house. There are a lot of man," explained Habiba opa. "Okay," she said and kept silent while holding Habibakhon's hand.

Dilbar couldn't forget her mother's head tied with gauze before her eyes. "Does it hurt?" she covered her face with her hand and started to cry again. Habiba opa scolded her, "If you cry, you will get sick. Go play with your friend, I'll cook something delicious. You guys keep playing." She thought the child would play and forget her woe. But Dilbar went to one corner and sit sadly. Seeing this situation, Habiba felt sorry for Dilbar. "Poor girl! She is thinking about her mother."

Fifteen days later, they discharged her mother from the hospital. Dilbar was always by her mother, then a cup of tea she brings then something else. It seemed she had missed her mom, and she didn't want to move away from her. Meanwhile, her uncle came with his children. At least for one day, there was joy in the house of Dilbar's. Risolat aya's head had been badly injured. Because of this, she often lost consciousness. Therefore, Dilbar's uncle strictly ordered that she should not leave her mother alone.

It got even worse for the poor little girl. Her mother also would faint away so often. In such case the girl hugged her poor mother tightly, because her uncle had ordered her to do so. This happened again one day when Risolat aya's sister-in-law Zulfiyakhon came with her husband to see her. Zulfiyakhon was afraid of this and insisted, "Dadasi,[17] we can't leave them alone, we will take my sister to our place." "Okay, we will consult the doctors there too," said Madaminjon aka.[18] It was really difficult for Dilbar until her mother recovered and got

---

[17] Dadasi – father of my children (a way of women addressing to their husbands)
[18] Aka – elder brother. Here added to show respect to an elderly man

back on her feet. Dilbar took on all the work with all her heart. Sometimes her uncle insisted they went to his place with them. Dilbar will never forget that day. Three or four days prior the the first of September, her uncle came in leading his daughter Odinakhon. Asking how she and his sister were doing he said "How are you? Are you feeling better know?" After sitting for a while, he took Dilbar and Odinakhon to the market and bought both of them the same school uniform, books, notebooks, and bags. Dilbar, who was happy about this, hugged his uncle tightly and said, "Thank you, my sweet uncle. She was grateful to her uncle for filling up her broken heart. Her uncle even bought a beautiful scarf for her mother. "I will make you some soup today," he said to cheer up his sister when he came home.

Dilbar, who was thinking about these things, alerted by the driver's loud voice saying, "Have something to eat!"

Tashkent was more beautiful than Holida said. Even Dilbar herself could not believe that she had come to such a big city and was staying there. Submitting a document was not easy either. With the help of Holida, they handed them over in the evening. After submitted the documents, however, a place to stay in was a problem.

Applicants were already settled. That day, she

stayed in Holida's apartment for a while. However, as the renting girls were going to the district where they were to practice, the tenant woman promised to give the flat to others. Therefore, Dilbar, with the help of a girl from Ferghana, found a place in a rented flat the next day. It was a bit far away.

It was the will of the Creator or had the creator pity upon young Dilbar for her hard work, she became a student. Dilbar's joy was boundless. There were ten more days before the start of studies. Many went home. Dilbar was confused, not knowing what to do. In fact, she had no relatives in Tashkent. When that Fergana friend said that she was going home, Dilbar also went to the bus station. Fortunately, she could get a ticket for the bus leaving at eight o'clock, so she went to one side and sat down in front of it, waiting for her friend Muruvvat, who said goodbye to Dilbar and went to the train station because there were no tickets left for buses to Margilon. Dilbar was overjoyed.

Dilbar, who arrived in Andijan at dawn, was in a hurry to go home. At the threshold, Dilbar was met by his mother. The joy of Risolat aya was boundless. Seeing her parents in good health, Dilbar couldn't hide her joy and cried. There were some people who we happy that Dilbar had been enrolled. Others thought how a poor man's child could go to university. But

Dilbar didn't brag to anyone that she had been enrolled and became a student, because she knew that no one would believe her. Dilbar said to herself, "How can I brag if I am a child of a poor, ordinary person?"

It had been almost three months since Dilbar had started studying. One day, when she was going to class, she was told that someone was asking for Dilbar. When she went out, she saw her brother in the courtyard of the dormitory! Dilbar was so happy! She thanked Allah for this. Now there was a brother who could look after her parents. The brother and sister did not let go of each other's arms for a while. Dilbar also missed her brother very much. His brother was quite weak, and he was very pale. Dilbar invited him to the room. But his brother didn't want to come in. "You go to your classes, I'll be around. Don't miss the class, we'll talk later." But Dilbar did not give up and finally took her brother into her room.

Brother, are my parents okay? They must have been really happy to see you? When did you come?" Dilbar buried her brother in the questions. The brother and sister talked with interest over tea. She ate with relish what his mother had sent her, especially tandoor[19] bread.

---

[19] Tandir – special oven for baking bread. It is heated with firewood

In the evening, her brother returned. "Stay for a couple of days, there is a separate room in the dormitory for parents who come from afar," said Dilbar. She wanted her brother to stay there. But her brother did want to stay.

"I have a lot of work to do when I go home. The apricot tree has dried up, so I'll cut it and store the wood in the cellar. I miss you. I wanted to see you first. If you don't go to class now, you will go to the market with me. I will buy you some things. May be a jumper and a coat. Soon it is winter and it will be cold. Dilbar was happy with her brother's words.

"Okay brother," she said. But first we will buy it for our mother. If you have more money, then you will buy for me too. Let our poor mother wear something new." The brother and sisters roamed the Charsu market for a long time. First, as Dilbar said they bought a beautiful woolen dress for their mother, a thick jacket, a thick coat for their father, a shirt, a sweater, a coat for Dilbar and many other things. She also bought a case that was popular at the time. Dilbar loved it. Although she claimed that her shoes were quite fine, he bought a pair of new boots for her sister. After the shopping, the brother and sister went to the kitchen to eat something. Dilbar was proud of herself, because she had a very strong brother by her side. "Dilbar, forgive me, sister. I heard how much trouble you had had because of me. You were very sick. Now don't think about anything, I'm here. Don't worry about home. I will take care of my father and mother myself, sister. Just think about your studies." Then he gave Dilbar some money. "Eat well, and if you don't have money, give a phone call to Inobat aya's house and I will send it by mail," he said. "Okay, brother," said Dilbar with tears in her eyes. After leaving the canteen, Dilbar begged him to stay one day, but her brother did not give up. He said that he had to go home and said goodbye to his sister. He headed towards the station. Dilbar got on the tram and went to the dormitory.

Dilbar was overjoyed as she was going to the dorm on the tram. Now she has a brother at home. Father and mother are not alone. Hard days are over. May her brother be wise. It was past three o'clock when she got to the dorm. Rano and Muruvvat were drinking tea.

As she put his belongings on her bed, she was embarrassed to see her friends looking at her with envy. In an instant, the three friends started looking at her things.

"Wow, look at this, Rano, I'll get it too. Is it good fit on me?" In fact, the jumper suited Muruvat very well. She was very proud of herself. Dilbar had not told her friends that her brother had been in prison. That's why she said, "My brother missed me. Today we will have pilaf," Dilbar said as she was placing down the things her brother had bought.

"Then I will switch on the gas stove before it's too late," said Rano. Since all other students were cooking at the same time, they had to wait because the gas stoves were not enough.

Days followed the months. Meanwhile, Dilbar visited her house a couple of times. Sometimes she was happy, and sometimes she was disappointed. Once when she was at home, her mother started talking about Lolahon. "I'm not sure, but I think your brother and Lolakhon have fallen in love with each other. What will people say? What if your aunt's words come true?"

That day, Dilbar took advantage of his brother's absence and came up to Lola opa.

"Opa, I am very much glad to have you here. You are like my real sister to me. You encouraged me in my difficult days. I heard something from my mother, is it true? Opa, I am not a young girl either. I got to this point with your advice and help. My father and mother are getting old. They need some care. If only I didn't study so far away. As you can see, I come every two or three months. Lolahon listened attentively to Dilbar's words and answered not hurriedly, "Dilbar, I also consider you to be my sister. It's true, I should have left this place the day your brother arrived. But I couldn't do like that, because I had promised you. I wanted to look after your parents as my own parents, so I was afraid that they would be left without enough attention. And now, I'm totally bound."

Dilbar, who was confused by Lolakhon's words, did not say anything to her mother. "Let my brother take care of himself," she said, comforting his mother. She went to Marifatkhon aya and gave her what she had prepared and got some more do'ppis. In her spare time, she used to earn money by sewing do'ppis, and did not receive money from home. The summer exams were approaching, so Dilbar quickly returned to Tashkent. She had asked for permission for three days.

"Today is the fourth day. I am still here because of Sunday," said Dilbar, who stayed at home because she wanted to make her mother happy, kissed her on the cheek and said goodbye. Her father prayed for a long time. Her brother followed Dilbar to the bus station.

"Brother," Dilbar said while saying goodbye. "I can't teach you wisdom, but think carefully yourself. Then don't regret it, you know our situation. Now I'm leaving with relief as you are here. My father and mother have no one to lean on except for us, think and act," said Dilbar.

"Okay, my sister, if you want me to behave well and not to get spoiled, you will agree with me. I have decided firmly."

At that moment, the brother and sister said goodbye to each other because it was time for the bus to leave. Dilbar's mind was buzzing until she reached Asaka. She could not understand her brother's words.

"If I can get a ticket earlier, I will call my uncle at home," she said to herself. It is good that there were few people in front of the ticket office. She went and stood in line. At that moment, she felt that a young man was watching her. She slowly looked back. She remembered this young man staring at Dilbar. She had bumped into him the dormitory in the yard on the day she started her university education. "Is he from these places?" Dilbar asked herself. After getting her ticket, Dilbar sat in the shade and wanted to know what time it was. She asked an old man sitting next to her what was the time. Along with studying, she started to continue her creative work. She made many friends. She became close friends with Rano and Muruvvat, who were living together with her in the same room. They did not even drink a cup of tea without each other. But no matter how happy Dilbar was, her heart still ached. She was thinking about her father and mother. She thought about their living and health. It is good that she had taken their neighbor's phone number. She called them every other day. When she knew that they were safe, she felt much calmer.

One day, when she called her uncle, his daughter-in-law picked up the phone as he was not at home. After greetings, she told Dilbar that her uncle and aunt had gone to Dilbar's house that day, that her brother was getting married to a neighbor woman, and told about all the things happening at home. This angered Dilbar again. And she was really upset with her brother. Couldn't he come to his senses? That was pretty low of him. Doesn't he feel sorry for their mother? Won't her parents see a wedding? Won't my poor mother see *kelin salam*?[20] Won't a virgin girl come through the threshold to their house? Dilbar was crying heartily. If she worked patiently for a year, he would earn money and get married. She cried so much that nobody could comfort her at that moment. She knew this and went to the foot of the dormitory yard.

No one passed through here. There she wept bitterly. The difficult days she spent, the bad things her mother heard from her sister-in-low, the days of having so little, everything started to come to her mind. What is going to happen? What about my poor little dad and mom? How

---

[20] Special traditional bowing of the bride

will they live in the neighborhood? How can I bear the taunts of my friends, "Serves you right, your brother got a wife with a child!" Dilbar talked to herself and not being able to find answers to her unanswered questions. She found solace in tears. When it got dark around, she slowly got up and walked towards the bedroom. But Dilbar's legs would not obey her. Perhaps it was because she hadn't had anything to eat since morning. She went to bed feeling a bit sick. Seeing her condition, Manzura rushed over and raised Dilbar and gave some tea to drink. She had a couple of sips, wiped her tears and lay down slowly. Her eyes were darkening more and more, and her head seemed to be spinning from lack of sleep.

Rano, who entered through the door, saw her friend's swollen eyes and felt that she was crying again. She looked at Dilbar with pity, but did not say a word. "She is in a difficult situation, I will not add anything to her situation," and remained silent. Dilbar still couldn't control herself, couldn't stop the painful tears that were still pouring from the bottom of her heart. In this state, she couldn't raise her head for a long time. She tried to find strength in herself, but it was impossible that moment. Seeing this situation, Rano came to her friend and said kindly, "Get up, my friend! Have a little snack. Otherwise you will get sick," and ran her hand across her cheek.

Rano felt so sorry for her that though she was an ordinary small girl and had endured so much grief. Dilbar found some strength and tried to get up. Now she wanted to cry out to kill her pain again, but some force prevented her from doing it.

"Dilbar, what do you want to say?" said Rano looking at her friend.

"Yes, comrade, let's go to the telephone box office."

"Okay. Have something to eat first, don't go hungry, Dilbar," said as the latter was trying to stand up. When the two friends went to the courtyard of the dormitory, Dilbar was envious of the student boys and girls who were happily talking on the benches. But none of these thoughts were interesting to her, she was thinking about her parents. "Maybe my mother is crying more bitterly than me." Even a cup of tea wouldn't go down her throat. "Hey! Brother, what have you done?" Dilbar did not even notice that she reached the telephone box. She gave the telephone number of her uncle to the operator girl and was about to sit down. Suddenly the operator called the Dilbar to the booth. She burst into tears when she as he hurriedly picked up the phone and heard her uncle's voice.

"Why are you crying, my daughter? Don't be

disappointed, that's called destiny. We have no choice. I Couldn't persuade. I made a small wedding party. My sister and my poochcha is proud. You don't think about anything. I will go to Tashkent in the near future. I will see you again. Don't think about anything, girl! Do you understand?

"Okay, uncle," she said. "Is my mother okay?" her voice trembled.

"Well, don't worry. My sister is happy." Dilbar, who came to her senses from her uncle's words, had no choice but to accept the fate, thinking that she would soon go on vacation and go home

\*\*\*\*

The student period of a person's life is the most exciting and memorable period. When you remember those times, a sweet pleasure appears in the heart of a person. It's like going back to happy, energetic times. At that time, the three friends were always together. They studied together and stayed in the same room. If they did not see each other, they missed each other immediately. Among her friends and among the girls of the group, Dilbar was distinguished by her politeness, simplicity, and openness. But her eyes always would be sad, as if she was constantly afraid of something.

She did not use say a single word that would hurt her friends' hearts, she thought about it and spoke not hurriedly and not loudly. Most of the guys in the group were not indifferent to Dilbar because everyone liked her habits. You could tell from the love letters left on the doorstep. But Dilbar was not interested in these letters.

Every time she went home, she would bring some do'ppis from that Marifat opa and she would sew them in her free time. However, she did not reveal her pains to anyone. She could be suffering much but nobody notised that. One day, when she was doing her homework with her friends, a song by that artist started to be played on the radio in the room. Dilbar, who was talking, suddenly fell silent and listened to the song so intently that she could absorb the song into her heart with all her being. Rano, who was initially oblivious, looked at Dilbar after the song ended. Her eyes were full of tears. Rano, who did not see Dilbar in this state, was confused by her condition, and asked her in surprise, "Does a person cry so much for a song?" Dilbar hurriedly wiped his tears,

"I don't know," she said, hiding her eyes.

Earlier, they used to listen to songs from the tape recorder that Rano had brought from home, but Rano, who had not seen Dilbar in this condition, started to be surprised. They always heard the songs of this artist, but Rano, who had not seen Dilbar in this condition, wondered what was going on or Dilbar felt sorry for. After that day, she started watching Dilbar. Every time she heard the songs of that singer, Dilbar's face became sad and her eyes filled with tears.

Rano fantisized that the song would have a serious effect on Dilbar, but decided to follow and watch Dilbar anyway. One day Rano hid the tape before Dilbar arrived. Returning from the lessons, Dilbar wanted to listen to a song and put on a tape recorder. But there was no cassette. She asked Rano, "No, I didn't see it," she replied. Not knowing what to do, she looked for it everywhere.

Rano was very interested in what her friend

would do when she can't find it. When she saw Dilbar's later condition, she regretted what she had done. Because on that day, Dilbar neither ate nor studied. Instead, she lay down and covered her head. Dilbar got up after a long time, his eyes were red from crying. Rano felt sorry for his friend. "Forgive me, friend," she tried to give the tape, but kept silent, fearing that she would be called a liar. She calmed herself with the dream that she would put it back in place in the morning.

However, Rano could not carry out her plan even in the morning, because Dilbar was already standing and writing something. The three of them drank tea together. Manzura started preparing to go to her classes.

"Dear Dilbar, are we going to be late for class." As if he hadn't hear what Manzura said, sat there until she reached a certain inner condition. Manzura began to urge her again, "Bulakol Dilbar, we will be late for class, hurry up!

"I won't go to the university today," she replied.

"Do you have any pain?"
Manzura's question remained unanswered. After Rano and Manzura went to class, Dilbar, who was alone in the room, pressed her face to

the pillow and cried. The more she envied her friends, the more helpless she felt. It is good that her brother's wife is fine. Whether out of fear of God or out of pity for them, she always lookes after her parents well However, thinking about her brother, Dilbar was depressed from inside.

In the meantime, her brother, who had had a child, started his misbehavior from a new. Lolahon was the daughter-in-law of their house with her two children. Dilbar thinking of these things didn't realize how long she sat in the bed. Finally, she got up and washed her face and hands and looked in the mirror. For some reason, she felt that her face was pale, and her eyelids were swollen from crying. Dilbar was very angry with Rano. No one else would get it from her, even if she got it, she should have asked for it. Munzura did no sense of songs at all. Or may be Manzura got bored of listening to the song and took it?

"I will buy a new one no matter what happens," she said. It was difficult because it was spring, and the weather on the street was changing a lot. When the tram arrived at the station, it started to rain. "I'm going to Chorsu!" She had received a scholarship the day before, so decided to send at least a little of it home by post, and got on the tram to Chorsu. Dilbar was gazing with envy at the rain hitting her window, and suddenly her thoughts were interrupted by a familiar voice.

"Where are you going to? I have got some business near here. Are you going to Chorsu?" Samad asked.
Dilbar said "yes", but then to herself "Why did I say that? How did he know I would come here? Okay, I'll get off when I get to Khadra, and I'll walk to it."

When the tram approached the stop of Hamza theater, she got up to go closer to the door of the tram. Seeing this, Samad said, "There is still time for you to get off. I have a business there too. Okay, good luck," he said, and got off the tram. After the tram moved, Dilbar crossed the road and started walking. First, she went to the communication department and sent money home to her mother. Then he bought a raincoat to protect herself from the rain. Then she bought a new cassette (tape) instead of the lost one and quickly returned. It was almost noon. "I should be in the room when in the room until my friends came home from class," she thought.

Even though Rano was physically in the classroom, her thoughts were on the cassette under the pillow in the room. Questions like

"What will I do if she finds it?! What kind of person will I be?!" haunted her. As soon as the lesson ended, Rana flew to the dormitory like a bird. She was putting her hand on the door handle when the song of that singer was heard from inside. After the thought, "She has found it!", shiver ran through her whole body. Rano, who barely opened the door and entered, put herself together when she saw a box of a new cassette on the table. She started asking questions as if nothing had happened.

"You have found it!"
"I bought a new one!"
"You didn't go to classes because of this cassette?" Rano asked, feeling sorry for her friend.
"Yes," Dilbar said and started laying the table. Then they together had lunch. Then Rano used the moment to ask Dilbar a question, "Dear friend, why are you sad? Why do you always cry? Are you sad to hear this singer's songs? Come on, my friend, you may get sick! You can trust me."

After a long silence, Dilbar told her each day that had passed. Dilbar started to wipe the tears that were washing her face as she finished her story. Rano was not happy that she had started such a conversation, and admired that her friend was carrying so many pains and sorrows inside. While Rano was also wiping her tears, she could not find necessary words to encourage Dilbar, to wait for her satisfaction. Finally, with difficulty, she found a word and tried to encourage Dilbar.

"Friend, take good care of yourself!" How beautiful you are! God willing, you will be happy! It is true that feelings can be so tender, but forget it! It is true that singer's song helped you, but this is the gift of creator! This is the reason."
"It's hard for me to forget," and she added after a long silence with a sigh. "This man's song brought me back to life. How can I forget! I will keep it in my heart forever." Dilbar seemed humiliated, in fact, she had so much respect for that artist, whom he had never seen or talked to, that it was difficult to express it in words. Dilbar, after gaining a lot of composure, turned her red eyes to Rano and said, - Please, my friend, don't let anyone know about it. Don't tell anyone!"
"OK," Rano didn't want to torture her friend who was already so sad. She promised sincerely, "Don't worry my friend, I won't tell anyone, but one question is bothering me. Even though so many days have passed, we have been together for three years, but you have not told us what is inside of you. If you had told me, maybe in your soul it would have been a

little easier? My friend, who has been suffering so much!!! Well, these days will stay behind, you'll see, there are better days ahead. Then you'll lough a lot."

Rano's words brought a smile to Dilbar's face. Both were silent. Rano was thinking of relieving her friend of this pain. And Dilbar was thinking about something. Ten-fifteen minutes later, Manzura came in. The new issue of "Saodat" magazine was in hand. "Dilbar, your poem has published published!" she happily gave the magazine. Dilbar, who was delighted by these words, said, "Really?!", and went to look through the magazine. In an instant, a beautiful smile took over his contented face. Rano, who was watching this, said, "Oh my friend! If only you knew how much laughter suits you?!"

Then the previous conversation and the pain were forgotten, and all three girls bent over the magazine. The poem was also very beautifully written. Now they were discussing the poem, and Manzura said, "Samad aka gave me the magazine. He said that you had gone to Chorsu, and asked me to give this to you when you come back."

Samad studied one course Dilbar's senior, in advanced traditional singing program. He had a crush on Dilbar from the first time he saw her, but he always respected her, never saying anything to her, and was careful not to offend her by saying something inappropriate. In fact, although something was felt from this strange attitude, no clear statement was heard. Even Dilbar herself did not know the reason for this high regard. Because Samad did not say his intention even once. In the language of the youth, he had not "confessed his love".

He was studying in the third year at that time. One day, Dilbar and Rano returned early from their classes. They both stretched out in their sbeds to get some rest. Then Dilbar asked for advice, "My friend, I wanted to transfer my studies to the part-time department and go to work."
"Why?" Rano could not understand this and immediately asked a question.
"After all, you know our family. My brother is still not coming home. Where does my daughter-in-law go to work with her young children? My father is old. My mother is also old. They can't do anything. I'm the only one they rely on. On top of that, suitors are coming to our house. You know. My father's and mother's dream is to see a wedding party of mine. I also don't want them to pass away with a dream unfulfilled. If they don't have other children, I'm depressed again thinking about them."

Rano's heart was also broken by Dilbar's words. She felt sorry for Dilbar. Because of this, the poor girl is always sad, but how can this little girl bear so many worries?! The clothes she is wearing are the same clothes that her brother bought her three years ago, and he has not bought anything else.

"Come to your senses, my friend, you studied so hard, it's not much left. You've been enduring all this, and there is a little more, my friend," she tried to say that, but Rano also felt sorry for Dilbar. When she went home, she used to sew the do'ppis that she brouht to sew until the end, he would take a little of her money and give the rest home. She would also send his stipend home. Rano had not seen that she used her money for herself. She washed and ironed a couple of clothes and wore them neatly. Dilbar again shed tears while talking about her life. She cried a lot. The two did not even notice that time had passed. At that moment there was a knock on the door. Both suddenly asked, "Who is that?" they stood up with a question. When she went to the door, "Dilbar, people from your house are asking for you!" came the voice of the superintended opa.

At this time, "Why do they ask?" What is it?" Dilbar was filled with anxiety. She did not realize how she got to the first floor. Dilbar hastily picked up the phone on the table. Lolakhon's voice came from the other side, "Dilbar, leave tomorrow, your father is very ill." After a few words, the phone was hung up. Dilbar now became more and more worried. Dilbar did not sleep until morning. She walked to and fro in the room. If only it were morning! Unfortunately, the night seemed to be so long. Finally, it was morning. Dilbar woke up early in the morning. Rano accompanied Dilbar so that she would not go alone.

Samad was waiting for them when they went downstairs.
"How did he know I was leaving?! Maybe it's Rano's work," Dibar thought and tried not to pay attention. He led them to the taxi standing next to the bedroom. Fortunately, they caught the bus to Andijan. They talked for a while while waiting for the bus to leave. Even then, Samad did not say anything. Only when the bus started to move, he said, "Okay, come on. Take care of yourself."

Days passed by. There was no sign of Dilbar. After almost a month passed, the librarian said that a letter had arrived in the name of Rana when she entered the library to do her homework and put the letter in Rano's hand. At first she thought it was from home. As soon as she saw the inscription "Dilbar" on the envelope, Rano was in a hurry to open the envelope and froze. Inside was an invitation to a wedding.

The following words were written in it, "Hello, my friend, Rano! How are you? Are you studying well? Rano, I'm getting married. I am getting married to a man I have never met in my life for the consent of my parents. They tried to transfer me. I could not say no. After all, I have to make their dreams come true! Their hopes are only connected with me. But now my world is dark. You know what it is. I couldn't love another person anyway, so it doesn't matter who they pass it on to. The love in my heart reaches me. Come to the wedding, of course. Your friend, Dilbar, who misses you." At that time, there were group members in the library. Rano did not know that Samad was among them.
"Girls! Look! Dilbar is getting married!" she announced this news to everyone. Everyone wished Dilbar happiness. "The bride is a lucky guy! A girl like Dilbar is going to marry him. May they be happy!" Everyone wished happiness.

At that moment, Rano's eyes fell on Samad. His pale in color. He was sitting quietly with his eyes fixed on one point. Even when in class,

Rano did not stop thinking about Samad. Why did he get into such a situation or did he love Dilbar? Why didn't he tell her if he loved her? The questions kept torturing her. She looked at the invitation and thought of Samad. As soon as the exit bell rang, Rano ran to the library. There was no one in the library, only Samad was sitting idly until she reached a certain point. Rano slowly came to him and asked, "Samad aka, what happened to you?"
Samad, who came to his senses from Rano's voice, looked at Rano and said, "Nothing happened." Then Rano, who saw that his eyes very young were confused. And Samad said, "Okay, I wish her a happy life!" he said and stood up and left.

In the morning, when Rano was leaving the dormitory, she bumped into Samad. "Rano, give this to your friend when she comes," he said, holding a letter in his hand. Rano received the letter and said, "Why?" she looked at Samad with a questioning look. He turned back and entered the dorm without speaking. Rano was surprised. She did not dare to ask anything. Rano never saw Samad after that. He stopped coming to university. They heard that he had gone home. About a month later, bad news spread in the dormitory. "Samad had a car accident." Now he can't even come to the university. His leg and arm got broken. These long-winged words immediately flew around the university. Everyone was surprised. Why did he drop it out? What is the reason? No one made it to the end. Only Rano seemed to know the reason. Was this an excuse? After class, she decided to come to the dorm and read Samad's letter. Why did he leave the letter? He didn't even come to study? And then these words. An idea came to Rano's mind, and she slowly opened the letter and read it, as if she would find the answer to everything in this letter. The following anguishing words were written in the letter.

"Dilbar, I wish I had written this letter to you earlier. But I was afraid of upsetting you. In fact, I fell in love with you the first day I saw you. My pain was inside me and I couldn't tell you. And now I'm sorry. You have become my dream. I couldn't sleep at night thinking about you, dark nights connected to mornings - all became a dream for me. Now my heart, which is in love with you, seems to be torn apart! If I hadn't met you, I wouldn't have suffered so much!

And now I curse the day I saw you when I fell in love with you. I don't even dream of this place where you don't study and you don't walk. I have no choice but to wish you happiness..."

When Rano was reading this part of the letter, she stopped and could not bear to read the rest of it. She put it under her pillow and started thinking deeply. "It's interesting! Why did he keep so many secrets inside?! Couldn't he say it earlier?! Is it so difficult to write on two sheets of paper!?" Such thoughts would settle in Rano's head and troubled her.

She did not even know how long she sat in this position. Once the door opened and Manzura entered, Rano's thoughts were shattered again.

That day, Rano could not sleep till late. Only Dilbar occupied her mind. In any case, she was thinking of going to see Dilbar and giving her the letter that Samad had given her. He fell asleep at dawn with this thought. He even saw Dilbar in her dream. She was sullen. Without saying a word, she wiped her tears and went away. No matter how much Rano tried to call Dilbar, her voice would not come out. She woke up in shock, was scared as if something had happened.

Whether it was motivated by a dream or because she missed her friend, in any case Manzura and she decided to go to see Dilbar. In the meantime, they wanted to sattle several times. Every time there would be an excuse and they would not be able to go. So a year passed. In the end, with Rano's behest, Manzura and Rano set out on the road. Two friends, hoping to find their friend with God's willing, got on the train saying "Where are you, Dilbar" and headed for Andijan.

As it is said, "who seeks will always find" and they found the house of the Dilbar's. They found it, but they saw not a very pleasant situation. Dilbar's father had passed away earlier that day. They stood at the beginning of the street for a long time, not knowing what to do. When they saw the women coming towards them, they followed them towards Dilbar's house.

After entering through the gate, Rano, standing among the mourners, looked for Dilbar with her eyes. When she found who she was looking for her heart was pulled back. "Is that Dilbar! It can't be so! I think I am mistaken," she thought. But Rano was not mistaken. That woman was Dilbar. Can a person change so much in a short time! She was very thin and her eyes were sunken. Her face was darkened and wrinkled on their temples because of weight loss. She also seemed to be aged ten years in this one year.

As soon as she saw Rana, Dilbar cried out. Rano, who knew the bitter and broken dreams of her friend, who was shedding tears while hugging Rano, joined her and cried bitterly. Dilbar was actually crying over her broken dreams and her miserable life along with the painful separation. Rano was ready to stand in this position to encourage her friend until she hugged her again, but there were many other women standing behind her. For this reason, the women entered the house in silence. After the prayer, the eyes of the women fell on these two girls.

"We don't know you yet, my daughter," said a beautiful woman who was quite a plumb one.

"We studied together with Dilbar. We have come to see her," replied Manzura. Then the women began to talk among themselves, "If only the poor girl could finish her studies like her friends, she would have some good job! Now she is working on the field. Risolat aya was in a bit of a hurry. She was thinking about her husband, so that he could see the wedding of his daughter!" said a woman.

"You are right!" added another. "The family where the poor girl is a daughter-in-law is a bit strict! May the creator make them wiser!

"Oh poor Dilbar! That's why she has lost weight! There is an omonat[21] of Samad on the other hand, as luck would have it. But it is impossible not to give it to her. He entrusted me with this omonat." Not knowing what to do, Rano was having much difficulty. "Okay, this

---

[21] Omonat – something given to someone in order to give to someone else

letter stays with me. Let this omanat be a big burden for me. I won't tell Dilbar. I'll say it after years, when I forget my pain, when I feel a little lighter, when my student memories fade away." Dilbar's voice from outside caught Rana's attention again.

"I am crying like your son, my dad!
I am crying like your daughter, my dad!"
She had such a distressing voice that not a single woman was left without tears in her eyes.

His son did not appear. He did not bury his father with his own hands. He was the only son.

"What happened to Dilbar's brother?" Manzura asked the woman sitting next to her.

"He started make the bricks of a big building in order to have Dilbar's wedding. When he asked for his money after the work had been done, the custumer did not give it having so many excuses. The wedding day had been agreed on the other side. He had no other choice but to go their again. When he asked for his money, the man quarreled. Not overcoming his anger, he beat that man, and was put jail for three years. Now he did not see her sister's wedding or her father's body. Tears came to Rano's eyes after hearing the woman's words. She then asked the woman, "What happened to Dilbar's wedding? What about the dowry?" asked Manzura. They tried to stop the wedding, but the groom did not agree. There was a wedding. "Poor thing, you were created only for suffering!" Rano couldn't hold back the tears in her eyes. After condolence, it was not possible to stay in Dilbar's house. The same day, they said goodbye and went to Margilon, to the Manzura's house.

It is true that life is like a river. Like water, it passes by without even letting you know. Thirty years have passed in the blink of an eye. During these years Rano often came to Tashkent. she met some of her fellow students, but it was not possible to see her closest friend, confidant, colleague Dilbar. It was not possible to meet her. Years later, after consultation with her husband, Rano moved to Tashkent from the neighboring country, Leninabad, placed her things and went to Bukhara to see her parents. The way is long. There were three other women in the taxi. The best thing is to chat!? May your companions be well on the long journey. The women in the car were charming too. Immediately the words fused together. Rano noticed that the women were from Andijan. Rano immediately asked them from which district they were, and got happy to hear the name of the district where Dilbar lived with her husband. As they say, "The one who goes to a mourning cries for their own pain", she started telling about her own problem.

"If I'm not mistaken, I have a friend in the district where you live. Her name is Dilbar. We studied together, lived in the same room, unfortunately, she could not finish her studies. Her husband's name was Komiljon, it seems.
"Oh, opa! Isn't that Dilbar opa from our neighborhood? She started on to describe her. Yes, yes!!! That's her!" Rano was suddenly happy as if she had found something precious. The woman did not know what to say about Dilbar and thought for a while.

"Oh, opa, don't say I told you, don't say you heard it from me. There is hardly any trouble she did not have during her life. Let me tell you that your friend is tougher than iron. I can even say that there is not a single day when she doesn't have some kind of trouble, poor woman! She worked in Russia and made a home with her young children. Until then, she lived in different rented flats with her small children. When finally, she hoped to live well, her husband went into debt in his job and sold everything. Not being able to overcome that disaster Komil aka got addicted to alcohol. They are now living next to us again. Hearing such things about her friend from those women, Rano got into a difficult situation again. "If so! My poor little friend! She came to this world to suffer!" Rano could not stop the tears coming from her eyes. The woman was embarrassed by what she said about Dilbar. Rano, who found her friend after such a long time, questioned the woman again, "How many children does she have?"

"She now has five sons. If they stand on their feet, Dilbar opa will be a rich woman. She endured all kinds of pain for the sake of her children, but I admire her patience!"

The woman kept talking, but none of her words reached Rano's ears. "My poor little friend!!! Do you have so much trouble onto your head?! Did you suffer so much because you sought parental consent? Did you come to the world only to suffer?!"

Then she asked the woman if she had Dibar's phone number. The latter couldn't say no as she looked into her companion's reddened eyes. "I'll find it for you now," she said and started dialing. After two or three minutes, a voice came from the other side.

"Assalomy Alaykum my dear Mom!"

"Hello! Are you all doing well? After the question and answer, the woman appointed her son, "You know Aunt Dilbar who lives on the second floor! So take the phone to her. Tell her that I want to speak to her." The boy was silent a little then said, "Okay".

About two or three minutes passed, and he said, "Hello, mom, here she is."

The woman spoke to the phone, "Hello, Dilbar

opa! A friend of yours wants to talk to you," and gave the phone to Rano.

"Hello," Rano had thought that she was calm, but it turned out to be still. "Hello, Dilbar!" from that side, "Hello! Who is this?" said someone.

"I am Rano," Dilbar's voice sounded as if something was stuck in her throat as soon as he heard the name Rano.

"Rano, my friend! Are you OK? How did you find me?" Rano couldn't stop crying, Dilbar was in the same situation. Thirty years of longing made them shiver a little.

"I've found you, my friend! I've found you! The Creator himself helped me to find you!" They did not talk for long. Rano told Dilbar that they had moved to Tashkent and asked him to come someday.

"My friend! Sorry, I'm going to Russia in three days. I may not be able to meet this time," said Dilbar. In order not to miss this opportunity, Rano said, "You will go to Russia via Tashkent! Come a day earlier, my friend, I'll take care of you myself. She talked and talked and finally convinced her to come and took Dilbar's telephone number.

Saying goodbye, he hung up the phone and with red eyes thanked the woman next to her. Rano returned from Bukhara so quickly that the people at home were surprised! She was happy at the thought of her meeting with her friend.

Rano, impatient, called the number in sent by Dilbar on the fourth morning. After hearing her friend's voice and saying that she was on her way, she calmed down and explained the address to the driver. Then she began to set the table for her friend. She kept on looking at the clock on the wall. "This watch means so many images! Time does not pass! Other times you will not have time to do something. Time does not pass while waiting. At two o'clock in the afternoon, the phone rang. Look-Dilbar!

"Rano, I'm here!" Dilbar's words remained in her mouth. Forgetting the phone, Rano ran downstairs. As soon as Dilbar saw Rano, she threw herself into her arms. The two friends did not want to let go of each other for a long time. After entering the house, Rano took a picture of her friend. Years had left their sign on her. Her hair was gray and her once beautiful face was wrinkled. The hard days of hardship were clearly visible on her face.

Dilbar also missed Rano very much! She did not want to be laughed at. She didn't even want let her go to fetch the tea, "we don't need the tea, my friend. Just sit next to me," she said, holding Rano's hand tightly. The two friends sat for a long time. They remembered the sweet memories of their youth. In the meantime, Rano took out a photo album that was like a gift from her student days. They watched the photos with interest.

Meanwhile, Rano said, "At least I will make dinner, my friend! You go on talking, I'll listen and cook," she said, and went to the kitchen. On the last page of Al'bom there was a letter from Samad. Rano remembered this and immediately came to Dilbar, "Comrade, this letter was for you. It has been waiting for you for thirty years," she said and put the letter in Dilbar's hand. She went to the kitchen again. Rano's hand was holding the skimmer but her eyes were looking at Dilbar.

Hearing Dilbar's voice, Rano immediately came to her. She was crying uncontrollably. A little later she slowly began to speak.

"I heard about Samad aka from Manzura, but I didn't know that it was like this," Dilbar looked at Rano sinfully, "I didn't even imagine that this happened to me. Say, Rano, what is my fault?! What's wrong with me?! He never hinted about it!"

"Dilbar, don't cry, I know he didn't say anything about it."

"My friend, I feel innocently guilty. Did he write this letter to me to make me feel like this.

"Dilbar, calm down, my friend," Rano was wiping her tears, - If I didn't know that it was an omonat, I wouldn't have given it to you. I didn't want you to suffer. That's why even when

I went to your house, I brought it back.

"No, my friend, you are to blame for this. You just gave the omonat! What could I do if he only told me?! I was very busy! You knew it!" Frankly, Rano did not expect this. She thought that Dilbar had forgotten all the pains and sorrows of the past. No! It is difficult for a person to forget!

"Rano, my friend! The Lord who created this world made it a kind of exam for me! In my childhood, I did not play and laugh happily like other children. I kept trying, hoping that maybe my future life would be better, but life didn't turn out the way I thought it would. I remember the day when you and Samad aka saw me off to the station like it was yesterday. When I came home that day, my father was really in a serious condition. My uncle, aunt and other relatives were at home. My father had tears in his eyes when he saw me. He blessed me for a long time. Three or four days later, his condition began to improve, but he was unable to stand. On the one hand, the old age, on the other hand, illness had taken away much of his strength. No one agreed that I should return to study. My brother didn't give up either, "Don't leave in this situation." I was helpless. About ten days later, my father's condition became much better. Then I said that I should not miss my studies. But no one listened to me. I had to stay again. The suitors came to us the next day.

My sister-in-law asked me to agree to this. I was caught between two grasses. My aunt (father's sister) said "You have to choose, either your father or your studies!" "If you don't need your father, you can leave now," she insisted.

I was helpless. I had to choose one. Either studying or my dad! Then I agreed to get married to please my father. And my studies ended from that day! No one had anything to do with me no matter how much I cried. Everyone got caught up in the wedding ceremony. I was helpless. "Have a Look at the guy you are getting married to," they said. I didn't want to. Because I was not interested in him. They sent my photo to the prospective groom.
Meanwhile, my brother started to make bricks for the construction of a big house to make money for the wedding. My poor brother, he did not come home even at night. He worked and stayed there. The wedding day was getting closer and closer, and my brother was not able to get the money he earned. We had quite little money with us. A week prior the wedding, my brother reluctantly went to that man's house again, but he didn't give the money and kicked my brother out. My brother couldn't bear it and hit that man on with a hoe handle and injured his back.

Hard days were with us again. My brother was

jailed up. He was imprisoned for fifteen days. Then he was tried and was imprisoned for three years. Now it was hard for me and my father and mother to bear this pain. Fortunately, my sister-in-law was honest, pious, and took all the work on her shoulders. The groom's family tried to stop the wedding, but the he himself did not let them. The wedding took place. My mother spent the wedding with tears in her eyes.

I thought I would live happily ever after. I was wrong! Again, painful days began for me. I was bride without any dowry. It's true! My mother did her best. They began to harass me saying, "She came without a carpet, and with only two velvet blankets," and saying that the dowry was little, but I endured whatever they said. For my mother! I hid it so that she wouldn't be hurt if she heard, but harassment started to be stronger and stronger. I didn't stop working from early morning until dark, field, house, big yard... I was not good even then!

Two years later, my brother-in-law got married. I got an Ovsin[22]. She was a daughter of a richer family. All the arguments started after that. I did not stop working with a small child in my arms. Even then I did not become a better daughter in law for them!

Dilbar recounted every day that had passed.

---

[22] Ovsin – wife of the brother in law

Tears in her eyes washed her face. Rano felt sorry for her.

"My poor friend! You have endured so much pain!"

I couldn't help bearing it. I couldn't go home... My father was happy to see my son and took him in his arms. I am thankful for that. Then he passed away when my son was six months old. His single son was at my father's funeral; he did not put his father to the grave with his own hands! Sometimes I wanted to give up, but I thought about my mother. I was patient with everything so that there would be no talks about us among neighbors. At such times, my husband would encourage me. He always said, "Be patient, everything will be fine", and I kept waiting for it to be fine. Rano, do you know, my friend, that when I was sick when I was young, I came back to life due to the song of a famous singer, and later I told you that I wrote a poem about him. On May 25, 1987, when I heard that khafiz[23] was going to give a concert at the Central Stadium in Fergana, I managed my poem to reach the hands of the khafiz via my friend who lives in Fergana. I was very proud of that then. Years later, in 1992, this poem was performed at the concert program held in the concert hall of Friendship of People on the occasion of the 550th anniversary of Hazrat[24]

---

[23] Khafiz – well known singer
[24] Hazrat – renowned person

Alisher Navoi. I was very happy about it. Even when I was facing difficult days in life, this man's songs helped me to be strong and patient. I received spiritual nourishment from his songs. I found the strength to live for my children."

Dilbar's voice got lower and lower and trembled. Seeing that, Rano, who was going to tell her about the dream she had seen, changed her mind. She didn't want to freshen her wound. They talked until dawn, as they had a lot to say to each other. Dilbar's tears did not stop talking about the past days. Rano joined her and cried bitterly.

"My friend! Even if you alone, you have suffered the suffering of a hundred women! Live well from now on, my friend! How is your family now? What about your children?"

"I am living in a rented flat now. There will be a house too, I hope!" Dilbar answered briefly, but clearly. She did not want to take up Rano's time to talk about her life again. Rano didn't ask more questions because she heard about her friend's life from the neighbor woman. She just encouraged and consoled her.

Dilbar hugged her friend as she set off in the morning.

"Thank you, Rano! I feel much easier now! Thanks for having you with me now!" Neither of them wanted to let go each other. Rano was thinking of encouraging her friend by saying

something. At last, after a little searching, she found some words, "Friend, do not torture yourself! You are a strong-willed woman! These days are also a test of Allah. They will soon pass. Your faith is strong. May your face be bright before the Creator after passing through divine trials, my friend! Don't forget me! Keep calling. This is a kind of help of mine. Use it for some need of yours," she said, giving three hundred dollars notes in her hand. Dilbar said, "That's too much. One will do." But Rano insisted and put the money into Dilbar's bag.
"What kind of a friend I am if I do not help you a little as a friend!"
"Thank you, my friend! I will pay you back in my better days. As the two friends say goodbye, Dilbar entered the train station, turned back and waved again. Her sad eyes remained before Rano's eyes.

"There are still two hours until the train leaves. I wonder if there are any cars going to Marhamat[25]? I would send this money home," Dilbar imagined that her wife would use it if he needed it with the children, so she went out. A taxi driver, who was calling clients to go to Andijan, came to her and asked, "Aka, is there a car from here to Marhamat?" He said, "Yes, my sister, this is the place where Marhamat taxis get their clients," and continued to call.

---
[25]Marhamat – a district in Andijan region

Dilbar said, "Thank you aka!" he didn't even listen to what she said. As he told the truth, there were three cars with tablets "Asaka-Marhamat" on. Dilbar slowly walked up to the older one and asked, "Aka, will you go to the marhamat?" she asked.

"Yes, sister, are you going there?"

"No, not me, I want to post some money to my husband."

"Okay, the postage is five thousand."

"Don't say that, take three thousand, please. I have little money. I am going to Russia myself. I want to give this to my children!" It seems that a person standing a little further recognized Dilbar, "You are the wife of Komiljon, aren't you" he said.

"Yes," said Dilbar happily.

"Give it to me. You don't need to pay any money. I will take it myself. Calm down, my sister, Komiljon is a friend of mine."

"Thank you, brother," taking the money out of her bag said Dilbar, "can you give it to my husband, please." Then she called home and said, "The father of my children, I am sending you some money. My friend Rano gave it. Keep using that. Also pay the rent. Use it until I send you more." The driver who heard this said, "Komiljon's business will get rolling, sister, don't worry, I'll deliver the money. Dilbar said to him, "Thank you brother," and went to the station.

In the train car, Dilbar was lucky to have a lower sit next to the window. "I will look around and not get bored." Dilbar's heart was full of sadness as the train started. "Now I will be away from my children again. I will not come until I have a house of my own. She kept in mind that she had decided with determination. As the train sped up, the city fell behind. Dilbar was looking into the distance, those difficult days began to pass before her eyes.

She was then pregnant with her second child. One day the big fluffy scarf of the new ovsin got lost. They searched for it several days. When they did not find it, they started to blame Dilbar for the lost. Even when she said "I didn't get it", no one believed her. Her mother-in-law even cursed Dilbar's saying, "If you have taken it, may the child in your womb not be born healthy." Dilbar, crying blood, did not know what to do. She was desperate when she could not convince anyone. She wasn't even called for food. Even if no one believed in Dilbar, Komiljon believed in her. He also told his mother several times, "She can't do such a thing. Do not slander her", but no one listened to his words.

After a few days Dilbar went into labor. Desperate, Komiljon called his mother at night. Ozodakhon opa came out immediately, "Who will continue to be offended at such an hour," she said, and quickly took Dilbar to hospital. Near the dawn, Dilbar gave birth to a healthy son like a ram!²⁶ Seeing his mother-in-law's joy, Dilbar forgot her insults. She calmed down thinking, "the truth will reveal itself."

After the birth of the second child, Dilbar's life became more calm. Many things were forgotten. It was already spring. One day, Ozodakhon opa saw Onorkhon, the younger sister of her younger daughter-in-law, in the market. Though the spring was approaching, the days were still quite cold. The scarf on Onorkhon's head looked somehow familiar, and she asked, "Isn't it Manzurakhon's scarf?" Unaware of anything Onorkhon answered, "Manzura sold it to me because it was too big for her." Then Ozoda opa said, "I mmade athief out of my poor daughter-in-law because of this scarf" and told Onorkhon the whole story. That day, when she came home, there was a big fight. Dilbar's sisters also apologized. But Dilbar was happy that the truth came out even more than forgiveness. She was glad that her reputation was clean. This quarrel became an excuse and her ovsin stayed at her parent's for four months. In the meantime, Dilbar was again responsible for the farm work and field work.

At that time, the cotton harvesting season was about to begin. Dilbar left her children in the kindergarten in the field shed and with the

---

²⁶ An Uzbek saying which means that new born child is healthy and big

women's brigade was clearing the cut cotton trees from the cotton to make way for the cotton harvester. Once her little sister-in-law came running and said, "Sister-in-law, a guest has come to our house. Go home fast." In her haste, Dilbar ran home forgetting his little son. If he didn't go quickly, he would be in real trouble from his mother-in-law. When she came home, she couldn't believe her eyes! His brother was sitting! Dilbar threw herself into her brother's arms. She cried aloud. Many years of dreams, longing, and anguish were crying together in this cry.

"That's it, I'm here. You won't be disappointed anymore. You are not alone, my sister!" said her brother, unable to stop himself from crying. Meanwhile, his brother-in-law also brought the children, "Your nephews are this big now, uncle," Ozodakhon joked. Tears filled his eyes as he held his nephews and pet them.

That day, when he was sitting at the table, his brother put one thousand soums in front of Dilbar, "Buy whatever you need, I will do the rest myself. Don't worry, everything will be fine." Dilbar, who had followed her brother back when it was time to say goodbye, she was overjoyed. Later she did the washing up. After cleaning the yard, she wanted to put the children to sleep because it was lunch time. Then his mother-in-law called her and said,

"We both will go to the market in the morning. At least you should buy a carpet for one house, my daughter, let's fix your house.

"Okay," Dilbar replied, handed the money to her mother-in-law and went into the house.

When Komiljon returned from work, it was almost noon. He was happy to hear that Dilbar's brother had arrived.

"Now you can walk happily. I told you that everything wuold be fine," he said in between. When Dilbar said that she and his mother-in-law would go to the market the next day, her husband got a little angry, "What did you do?! How do you know what condition he is in?! He gave it, and you took it?" Ozodakhon opa, who was listening to these words, intervened, "What's wrong? It is his task to give. Look at the house of my poor daughter-in-law. I will buy the necessary things for the huse tomorrow. After his mother's words, Komiljon said, "Do what you want to," took his son and walked out.

In the morning, the mother-in-law and the daughter-in-law set off to the market. When the day was approaching noon, they filled up one taxi and came back.

Dilbar overjoyed! They threw the things they had bought onto the so'ri. "Even if we bought so many things, we still have more than two hundred soums left over."

In an instant, Dilbar's house became like a normal one. Ozodakhon opa was also happy, "Now, if a guest comes, he will enter your house."

Dilbar's life was now on track and she was living with gratitude for the day she saw. One day, it was cotton picking season, when she came home, she saw that her ovsin had arrivedt. The mother-in-law said that Dilbar's ovsin said, "I won't fight with my ovsin anymore." Dilbar was also happy about this. Friendship is the best of all!

"My dear mom, I am also alone. It's good if we are like sisters!"

"Manzurakhon also said so," her mother-in-law was happy too. In the meantime, her ovsin came out of the house:

"Wow! Stop! I didn't know you came," she said, opening his arms. Dilbar also hugged her strongly, "We have missed you," she said jokingly. They prepared food with all sorts of jokes to each other, but Manzura did keep what she said. A week later, she began to provoke from anew. Again, Dilbar slowly began to be seen negatively.

After her jvsin returned home, Dilbar's peace was disturbed again. Inevitably small quarrels began to increase with the excuses of "my sister-in-law said, my sister-in-law did". Even his children could not walk freely in the yard.

His mother-in-law did not like Dilbar's honest words. Those days were the last days of December. As the work on the field and at the yard was almost over, Dilbar asked for permission to go to mother's home.

"You went to your Mom's home recently. Let your ovsin go this time. Her mother is ill. You will go later," said Ozoda opa trenchantly. Not knowing what to do, Dilbar had no choice but to say "okay". While Dilbar was kneading the dough, Manzurakhon came up to her and said,

"I could have done it myself. You are doing this to denigrate me. You have got an evil heart! Don't be too much proud with the things your brother bought for you now!" Dilbar, who did not expect such words from her ovsin, did not know what to do.

"Manzurakhon, I have no such an intention. What do you mean? If I have something, it's like everybody has. My brother bought it for me."

"Yes, I know, he bought it with the money he had stolen. I heard. He may also steal ours when he comes, that thief!"

Dilbar could not bear this. Now he was about to speak, but stopped when seeing her mother-in-law at the threshold.

"Okay, I'm gone. Look after my house, so that

thieves do not steal everything!" Dilbar left with a curt speech full of irony. Not knowing what to do, Dilbar wanted to tell his mother-in-law everything. After washing her hands covered with dough, entered the house where her father-in-law was sitting and looking after her playing son. Meanwhile, his mother-in-law also came in, "I have heard everything. Well, don't be offended! This daughter-in-law of mine is so impertinent. Hold on. We will build you a separate house. Dilbar, who was greatly uplifted by his mother-in-law's words, wiped her tears and went to the yard. It was a long time before the barn came back to sweep the sides and feed the cattle. When she was coming home after washing her face and hands, she heard the words of his mother-in-law who was rocking the cradle, "She said, 'I won't live her if you have this daughter-in-law of yours.' I'm dizzy. What is wrong with this poor little thing? She hates her it so much!" Standing at the threshold, Dilbar did not know what to do. She slowly walked towards the door, entered the kitchen under the pretext of dough.

"The dough is ready," she said to herself. Ozodakhon opa came out when the the fire in the tandir was burning for the bread to be baked. But Dilbar did not dare to look in the direction of her mother-in-law, because she did not want to show the tears in her eyes. During lunch, her mother-in-law noticed that Dilbar was crying at the table,

"Does a person cry for everything? Tell me yourself. You're going to listen to this forever!"
It was a kind of adding insult on injury for Dilbar was ready to burst into tears.
"When did you go home?"
"At the end of September. After my brother came."
Davronboy ota[27] glanced at the old woman. Since then, the younger daughter-in-law has been at her mother's home three or four times. Dilbar was about to say this when her father-in-law stepped in.
"She could have stayed, and this daughter-in-law of yours could visit her mom. She must have missed her mother too! Be equal to two of them!

Sister Ozada burst out, "What am I doing not being equal? Eh! You keep talking without knowing. She also insisted that she should go today. What do I do?"

"That is all right, dad! I can go later. Dilbar tried to ease the situation."
The next morning, when Manzura arrived, Dilbar was allowed to go home. Her father-in-law gave five soums of money saying that she would buy something for the children. As soon

---

[27] Ota – father, sometimes elderly and respected man

as Dilbar caught the money, Manzura started, "Yes, they won't give me a penny while I'm leaving."

"You can stay there three or four days," said her mother-in-law while seeing her off. Traveling with two children is not easy. Walking up to the big stone path. Long she was carrying a child in one hand and leading the elder son in the other, with a bag on the shoulder. Even going home was a pain. After going to the center, Komiljon was called from his workplace. He carried his son to the bus. "I will go and bring you home myself," he said while they were leaving. She wanted to say what happened the day before, but she didn't want to upset her husband either.

When Dilbar came home, she was very happily. Her sister-in-law, Lolakhon was also very pleased. She does everything according to her sister-in-law's wishes. She said, "You rest! You have a lot of work. Gather strength," she did not go beyond these words. She also took care of Dilbar's child.

From there on, both Dilbar and Risolat Aya's spirits rose like a mountain. At the dinner table, Dilbar told Lolakhon something that had been on her mind for a long time, "My dear sister-in-law! Thank you! You haven't said a single harsh word to me or my mother in all these years. You treated me like your own sister. Even when my brother was gone, you did not shed a single tear from my mother's eyes. You made her dearer than your own mother. Praise be to God who gave you to us! Thank you my dear sister-in-law!" Dilbar wiped her tears and her heart was full. Her mother also blessed her daughter-in-law for a long time with tears in her eyes. "Look at my nephews, they are so cute!" said Dilorom looking at her eldest nephew.

"Aunty, my daughter Dilorom will go to school this year," said her mother proudly, "Look how time is passing. Recently she was e small girl. Conversing enthusiastically, they didn't even notice that it was late.

On the third day of their stay, Dilbar, who had regained her composure at home, prepared to leave. After lunch, she also prepared her children. Even though it was late, there was no sign of Komiljon. "Perhaps he has a lot of work and doesn't have time, so we will go ourselves," said Dilbar, but her brother was against. He said, "Now I will take you to your place myself, in a taxi." He said, "Wait a minute" and left.

When Dilbar reached home, it was dusk. Her brother let them in through the gate and said goodbye and went away as the taxi was waiting.

At the threshold, Dilbar was confronted by her brother-in-law. He passed even without saying hello. Dilbar's heart was troubled by this act of his. She did not doubt that something had happened. As soon as she entered, she felt that her father-in-law felt nauseous.

"Assalomu alaykum, are you doing well?" she said softly. No one even responded to her greeting. The eldest son caressed her grandfather. The grandfather smiled and said, "Have you come?" said loudly. Only the mother-in-law stood up and met her daughter-in-law and took her child by the hand. "Didn't your son come?" Dilbar asked, and after that she didn't say a word.

"Maybe he is drinking somewhere. Making himself happy. These people have nothing to do with anything. The day has passed," added her father-in-law. As it was a cold day, she left the children and wanted to light a fire in the stove. On the way out, the older ovsin, "There is no electricity in your houses, sister," she said.

"Near the oven there is an oil lamp. You can use it, said her mother-in-law bitterly.

"The oil lamp doesn't have any oil inside," she said to her ovsin, who was cooking in the oven.

"I have nothing to do with it?! It serves them right!

"Manzurakhon, I am talking to you normally. If I say hello, you won't accept it. I'm older than you anyway!" she went silently to the house of Komiljon's grandmother and asked, "Granny, can I have your candle. The house is dark. They say there is no electricity. Ayimkhon Aya told the story of what happened while she was giving candles, and she said, "Go to your house quickly." Dilbar was about to enter the house when Kamiljon came. He did not see Dilbar in the dark and went into the parent's house. Dilbar, who did not dare to enter, immediately after her husband entered their own house. She wanted to put a candle on the stove, but the stove was not there.

"Where is the stove! Does Komiljon know? What if there is another quarrel if I tell him now! What do my children do in the cold?

What are their goals? When Dilbar was looking for answers to her questions, her husband came through the door carrying their son, "Hold on for now. I've found a house. We are moving tomorrow. There was a fight yesterday. That's why I didn't go to fetch you. I will never make my children orphans. I will not divorce you. Komiljon said these words with some force. Meanwhile, they were called for food.

"If they say something, don't talk back. Hold on. Let's go out of here quietly." At that moment, Dilbar felt very sorry for Komiljon. "He is ready to do anything for us!"

"No! Why should talk back? I didn't fight with anyone!"

"Okay, go."

"You go with children; I will catch up. When Dilbar entered her motsher-in-law's house carrying her child, everyone was busy eating. The eldest son is busy eating next to her grandfatsher, who has nothing to do. Dilbar also sat at the corner of the table. Now she reached for the food. Her Ovsin got up, closed the door and left. Not knowing what to do, Dilbar put the food she had in her hand into her mouth, but it was difficult for her to swallow it, because her mother-in-law also followed her younger daughter-in-law.

"Wshen will there be peace in the house?!" shouted her brother-in-law. Drive her away! How long more will she frown!? What is wrong with my poor sister-in-law? You have spoiled her calling the daughter of Maqsim[28] aka . Everything is for her! If I speak a bit more, I will be in trouble!" he also left angrily. Dilbar regretted going into the meal.

Not knowing what to do, Dilbar slowly got up and went out carrying her child. She heard some shouting coming from her Ovsin's house

---

[28] MMaqsim - Religiously educated person

only when she went to the door. She knew that Komiljon was there too from his voice that she could hear. "If I vacate the house, will you leave me in peace?" Dilbar did not understand to whom he was saying those words, but she knew that it was about them.

"Didn't I fit in my father's house?" His voice sounded like a cry.

"My son! Don't say that! You will fit!" It was the voice of Oyimkhon ena[29]. Manzurakhon was shouting even stronger. It was cold, and Dilbar did not know what to do with the boy. Then her father-in-law came out, "What's going on?"

"I don't know, dad, they are shouting. After her father-in-law left for his daughter-in-law's house, Dilbar entered her own house. The girls had already tidied the table.

"Hold your brother. I will do the washing up," she said to one of the girls.

"Are going to do the washing up even if you didn't eat?" Mavluda asked childishly.

"What's wrong with it? It was you who ate. I can do the washing up," she said jokingly. He was taking out a pile of dishes when she bumped into her motsher-in-law and said, "Wow." Komiljon came to her while she was washing the dishes by the stream.

---

[29] Grandmother

"Dilbar, it seems that we cannot stay here. You understand! Put together everything in the morning. We move in a new place with only some belongings. When we get a house later, we'll take the rest. Now it seems that there is no peace for us. Manzura's ring is missing. I don't want them think you are to blame for that!

"I wasn't at home!" - Dilbar's heart was full. "Why am I to blame for everything?!"

"That's why I say let's go out, thinking of you! Today you sleep at my mother's house with the children. Our house is cold. Children should not catch a cold."

Dilbar, who had put her children to sleep, was startled by the shouting in the yard.

"Granny, what's happening again? - Ayimkhon was about to get up, "don't go out. It is cold outside. I will look," as soon as she went out to the yard, Komiljon's voice came, "Hit me, hit me until you are satisfied!" Dilbar threw herself into the yard. She ran and tried to separate the brothers, but she could not. The brothers fought each other like strangers. Dilbar clung to her husband with all her might. "You don't hit him! He is Your brother!" She didn't listen to the words, but she didn't want to stay either now. They took Komiljon's brother into his house. Dilbar and Komiljon were left alone. Seeing the blood on her husband's face, Dilbar immediately ran to fetch some water. Meanwhile, their uncles (father's and mother's brothers) also arrived hurriedly. One of them who saw the blood on the face of Komiljon said, "Idiots!!!" and went inside. When she entered the house, their uncle was shouting. "What happened to your dogs? Who says you were born to the same parents!? Shameless you are!" The uncle who came to the end after asking everything, said gently, "Komil, you are older, he is young. Don't be upset! It will be forgotten soon!"

"Uncle, I will leave in the morning! Everything is decided! I can't live in this place."

His voice trembled, his heart was full or because of the cold his voice was trembling. The more responsible it was to keep the family, the harder it was for Komiljon to leave his parents' house. But he was forced to go to a rented flat because of family disagreements. However, Dilbar did not want to leave the house. "Why, stop it, the father of my children! I will endure," - she said many times. But she could not convince Komiljon. After that, Dilbar collected everything in the morning. She prepared everything to leave.

The next day around noon, Komiljon brought a car. When she was carrying her luggage, neither her father-in-law nor her mother-in-law said anything about what she was doing or where she was going. Isn't it a village? All the neighbors gathered. Elders said, "Wshere will you go, in the frost of winter? Look at your children! Come back, my son!" And some said Those who said, "Don't cool down your hot place!", but Komiljon said, "I can't go on living like this." Turning to his father said, "Pray, father!" But his father did not pray. Tangrikul ona, who was over eighty years old, saw Komiljon with tears in her eyes and said, "Here, I am praying for you, my son," and everyone opened their hands for a prayer. He prayed for a long time. As the car was moving, Komiljon cried with bitter tears in his eyes, "Father! Say goodbye to me!" he said.

From the day he arrived in a new place, his responsibilities increased again. Rent payment, children's food. Cold on the one hand. No gas, need for firewood! Now difficult days for Komiljon began. He went to work in the morning. After coming home from work, with the permission of the neighborhood elder, he pruned the maples on the street and made firewood at night. Sometimes his hands were frozen and could not even hold the ax. Even in such difficult days, he never complained. "It's okay, the mother of my children, these days will pass!" he said to cheer up Dilbar. Once, her younger son was very sick with a cold. One day when she was visiting the doctor, she saw a woman selling do'ppis while passing through the market. She went forward and asked for help saying that she knows how to sew doppi ornaments.

"Okay, girl, come to my house later," the do'ppi seller said. While explaining her home address, she said that her name was Maharramkhon. When her husband came home from work, she wanted to leave her son with him and go to do'ppi sellers place. Her husband was against this idea.

Stay at home and look after at the children! We will earn our living somehow," he said.

The father of my children, I can do this. I'll help you. It will be very difficult for us from one salary of yours to the next. Don't say no! Her house is not far. I will come right very soon." Komiljon, who was helpless, said "OK". It was good that she brought some do'ppis to be sewn. She sewed ten do'ppis in two days. Giving each of them by two soums, she earned twenty soums. Maharramkhon praised Dilbar as she liked her work, "If you do such a job, I will not give it to another sewer, I will give it only to you," she said. When she came home, Dilbar was happy and gave the money to Komiljon.

"If you use it for the shopping tomorrow, we would be able to reach a little further. If we get the money for the next work, we will pay it for the rent. It is good for our living."

It was spring not before long. Meanwhile, Dilbar found a job. They sent both of their sons to kindergarten. Dilbar became an assistant to her husband. What one earns was used for the household, and the other one's earnings were saved. As time went by, everything started to be put into its place. In the meantime, Dilbar's ovsin Manzura got completely divorced with her husband. She apologized for the slander and bad deeds she had done to Dilbar, whose sisters-in-law also often visited them. Because Dilbar had not say bad things to any of them, she treated her sisters-in-law in the same way as before. But she could not forgive Manzurakhon, because she could not forget all the troubles she had done to Dilbar. She heard so many insults, and saw many difficult days!

Considering the condition of the family, one of the houses being built by the city administration was given to Komiljon. Of course, this was greatly helped by the Post office where he worked. Their live was steadily improving. For Dilbar, it seemed that the difficult days were behind her. Meanwhile, the house given was on the first floor of a two-story house. They recovered a lot by their own efforts. One day, when Dilbar came home from work, there was tandir bread and some other staff from the village on the table. When she asked who brought it, the children answered, "One uncle". When she was trying to find out who it was, Komiljon came out of the bathroom.

"Who's was here, the father of my children?" Dilbar said curiously.

"My father and mother," said her husband happily.

"Why didn't they stay?"

"We are leaving tomorrow."

"Why?" said Dilbar hurriedly.

"I don't know, he said some kind of ceremony."

"I can't go. You go yourself."

'No, don't do that. Let's go together. After all, They ARE my parents! Desperate, Dilbar had no choice but to say yes."

Life went on like the water of a stream, hitting from stone to stone and sometimes flowing silently. No matter how hard times Dilbar saw, her life was full of humiliation and dreams, she never complained, she lived believing that better days would come.

Sometimes, even in the days when she was in need of bread, she did not expect help from anyone, she could not find words other than to thank the Creator for her fate. Years passed after months.

In the meantime, Dilbar's mother also passed away. Now Dilbar was completely alone. She didn't feel lonely when her father died because there was her mother. But after her mother's death, she was felt to be lonely in such a way that it is difficult to describe it in words.

During her lifetime, her mother kept saying to her daughter and son and brother, "If I die, put my body next to my parents." It was New Year's Eve. Dilbar, who came from work, was happy to see her mother. And the children were around her. One after another were sitting on her lap. Seeing that they were happy, Dilbar didn't even say "Be quiet" because she was happy to see her children happy. Two days later, Risolat aya was about to leave despite Dilbar's begging, "Stay some more." Komiljon called a car. While saying goodbye, looking at Dilbar, she said, "I will spend the New Year and go to your uncle's house. You go tshere."

Dilbar, who had sent her mother, was a bit heartbroken. 'Why did she do that? Did I say something inappropriate?!' She could not understand.

Komiljon, who took her mother-in-law and returned home, was also surprised. "Why did she do that? Are we disappointed in our work?' But neither of them could find the answer, "Okay, the day after tomorrow is the new year. I will go and get news," said Dilbar. Because it was a day off, she went to do laundry.

After washing the laundry, she bathed her children. Tomorrow they will go to school and kindergarten. Because of those small things to do, she forgot her troubling thoughts about her mother. Late in the evening, an unexpected news that came shocked Dilbar. "Why has she got ill?" asking herself that question, she didn't even know that she reached her mom's home. When she entered the house, her uncles had already arrived. Seeing Dilbar's arrival, Risolat opened her eyes and asked, "Have you come?" and closed her eyes again. Seeing her situation, Dilbar felt as if something broke inside her. "Why did her mother end up in this situation?" She was looking for an answer to the question she asked herself. Her uncle said "I will take my sister". This made Dilbar even more worried. Her uncle did what he said and took Risolathon aya to his place.

"Dilbar, you go home. You will go to see your mom in the morning. Look at your children," said her uncle as they were leaving. Then Dilbar entered the house, the house where her mother used to sleep was deserted. Dilbar, whose heart was full, cleaned up the room.

"Sister-in-law, I'm leaving," she said to Lolakhon, who was walking in the yard. When Dilbar entered the house, the day was coming to an end. At home Kamiljon was eating with her children:

"Is she okay?" Dilbar said "Yes," and started crying.

"What will I do if something bad happens?!"

"Hey! Speak about good things. She will be all right." But Risolat aya did not go well. Ten days later she left this world.

After her mother passed away, Dilbar was very restless. Because she was very attached to her mother. As if time heals everything, the pain of separation gradually disappeared, even if it was a little while she was busy with her home and children. Years later, their lives were normal again.

One day it was a special day – professional day of Communicators. In the morning, seeing off her husband to work, Dilbar, who was overwhelmed with household duties, did not even know that time had passed.

At that time, she was on maternity leave after the birth of her fifth son. In the evening, a man named Abdulhokim, who worked with Komiljon in a car, brought him drunk and handed to Dilbar a stack of papers and a gun, "Be careful and put it in a safe place. You will give it to him in the morning when he regains consciousness." But there was no money. Komiljon, who came to his senses in the middle of the night, first looked for the money. Dilbar said "Here it is in the wardrobe."

"Didn't he give anything else" Kamiljon, who was confused, said, "There was money! A lot of money!"

"I don't know?" he left without even listening to what she said. Dilbar's heart was filled with confusion after the arrival of her husband an hour later.

"What happened? Where did you go?' But there was no answer to that question of hers.

Komiljon, who went to work the next morning, took on a huge debt. That money was lost without a trace. He was not alone then. When Komiljon went to every post office and distributed pension money and as a holiday bonus money, they said that it was a holiday and asked them to drink. Having had more than enough Komiljon lost his consciousness, could not remember whether he had distributed all the money or not. There should have been a receipt when it was distributed. So, that was it, that was it, and the money was gone. Two days later, Dilbar went to the head of the post office.

"Sister, if you don't put this money in place within five days, Komil aka will be put to jail. I am not writing a statement against him because of your small children. Do your best," he said.

Now difficult times for Dilbar began again. "Where can we find so much money in such a short period of time?" After thinking about it, she started selling household appliances. Even if she sold everything, even their flat, they would not have collect so much money. Desperate, Dilbar started looking for a loan. It was impossible not to put the money in its place. Time was running. "We have to pay the money in five days. There was a note saying that if we don't pay, we agree him to be taken to the court. Dilbar was trying to find money no matter how difficult it was. There was no one left whom she did not ask for a loan. In any case, ninety thousand soums had to be paid.

Desperately, she went looking for money again, now the important thing for Dilbar was that her husband was not arrested. Their children could not be called the children of the imprisoned guy, but there was no one who would give them money either. Not knowing what to do, Dilbar went to his father-in-law to be saved. She knew that nothing would come out of them, even if they had cattle and sheep, but she did not despair, but went to them, hoping that they would help their son. But she returned with a thousand regrets.

"Don't sell the house, your children will be on the streets again. He is to blame himself. Let him suffer it himself," her father-in-law said and got up. Desperate, Dilbar returned home. In those days, her father-in-law bought for his younger son a brand new car. The thing that hurt Dilbar the most was that they both were their sons!

That day, she began to sell everything in his house: carpets, furniture, everything she had bought for the family's livelihood. But still a lot of debt remained. Even then, the money she said was not enough. She sold everything, even the dishes. Even then, it was barely worth sixty thousand.

It was raining. Dilbar was again looking for money, but who would give it? There was no one left whom she did not ask for money. She was in such a state that even the pouring rain did not affect her. Her father-in-law's voice was still ringing in her ear. Once she came across Namunakhon, who was also engaged in business at that time. Seeing the situation of Dilbar, Namunakhan asked, "Are you OK? What is this walk for?" Dilbar's heart was full. She cried and told about what happened. Namunakhon listened to her story carefully and said, "Go home now. Do not walk in the streets like this. You will get wet through. I will visit you soon," she said and made Dilbar go home.

An hour later, Namunakhan brought ten thousand soums.

"You will give it back when you have it, use it without embarrassment." Dilbar's eyes were full of tears. Now she wanted to hold Namunakhon firm in her arms, but she couldn't even raise her arms.

"Thank you, comrade! This deed of yours will remain in my heart!"

"I am proud of what I have done! These days will pass!"

Dilbar entered the house and counted the money again. "I have to take it tomorrow. Where can I find the rest?!" The poor woman was depressed again thinking about her children.

"What do they do now, there is no house, no goods! Where shall we sleep?" Dilbar, who could not stop the tears pouring from inside, cried for a long time. Seeing this situation, her children surrounded her. Looking at them, Dilbar, who was even more crushed, got up. Komiljon was crushed, unable to eat a meal or even a sip of water, "It's only my fault!" he said.

Suddenly, her brother came in. They thought he was unaware of anything. Dilbar did not know how to start the conversation, Tursunboy himself started, "Now I hear everything in the post office. There is no need to hide. What did you do my dear brother-in-law? My sister, isn't made from iron!

"Brother," Dilbar wanted to interrupt.

"You don't say anything! Look at yourself! You have never seen a day. Another pain?!

"That's right, brother," Komiljon said with a sinful look, bowing his head. "I didn't expect it to happen either." Seeing the color of Komiljon's face, it seems that Dilbar's brother felt sorry for him or understood the situation.

"I have no salvation now either. I will bring what I can in the morning." Komiljon got up and comforted his sister. When she followed her brother out and came back, her husband was sitting on the floor with his head between his hands.

"You also having a hard time, aren't you?

"The mother of my children, it was better that I was locked up than I showed you this day!"

"Don't say that, the father of my children! You will see these days will pass away, we'll forget all about it. This is also a test of the creator! We've lived together for sixteen years. How many difficult days we have seen! This is one of those!" said Dilbar.

The next morning, they added the money brought by her brother, all together eighty thousand. "I can't stand this fat anymore!" After placing the money in a big bag, she went to the post office carrying a heavy bag with her second son, Dilshodbek. It was raining in the street. By the time she arrived at the post office, she was freezing. As soon as she entered the door of the room, Dilbar burst into tears. It was a cry of grief because of the lost family and their children who were left on the streets without any care. Here, Dilbar was met by the head of the Post office. Then she came up to the deputy, the cashier and the accountant. They placed the money on the table and counted twenty-five, ten, five, three, and one soum notes separately. Then they received the one by one according to the act.

"A little over ten thousand sums not enough," said the cashier, looking at Dilbar with an evil eye.

"I will not pay even one more soum. I have no choice. Understand my situation! God sees who is being paid for the money. "May him get his punishment," said Dilbar, crying. Then the chief said, "Okay, sister! Don't be upset!"

It was already late in the day before they turned the conversation around and handed over the money. Dilbar cried until she reached home leading her son. "What should I do now?" How can I pay off the debts? If only my children were young!" She knew that her legs were very tired only when she entered the house with a thousand thoughts in her head. On that day, her brother had done a lot of shopping. Until Dilbar arrived, Komiljon had prepared a meal, but no food would go down her throat! She forced herself to eat a little. At that moment, she felt that her body temperature had risen.

Dilbar went to bed and lay for three days without raising her head. When she tried to get up, her body throbbed and hurt like someone who had been beaten. In the evening, her mother-in-law Ozodakhon came. When she saw her condition, she felt sorry for Dilbar. With slow restraint she said, "it's no use lying like this. Get up and try to pay off the debts now. The postman went to the neighborhood yesterday and distributed people's pension. She did not give us our pension. They withheld your father's and my pensions. We only get a pension of three hundred soums, and it is gone. Something stuck in Dilbar's throat from the words of her mother-in-law. It was not possible for her to talk about the money. For your child, that money could be used as a help! Dilbar's heart was full again. She forced herself to stand up. She entered the bathroom to wash her face and hands. When she looked at the mirror in front of her, she was afraid of herself! In front of Dilbar, who had not looked in the mirror for several days, there was a thin, pale woman! Seeing herself in the mirro, Dilbar felt humiliated.

Dilbar got up early in the morning. "I'll continue to lie if I don't find some strength to get up," she said, and went to work after breakfast. She had not been able even to go to work for several days. She seemed to be a little distracted at work, but she remembered those debts and was thinking about how to pay them. Dilbar, who was walking with her dream all day, did not notice when she came home late in the evening and wandered in the streets day and night. Now it was noticeable. No matter how much pain she suffered, she tried not to make her husband feel it. "We women cry and feel better. A man's pain is inside!" She was afraid that she would get sick again.

Soon the lenders began to ask for their money. It was difficult for Dilbar, who did not know what to do now. One day one of the lenders came and spoke harshly. All her neighbors heard it. Dilbar, whose face was red from embarrassment, did not know what to do and stood for a while as if rooted.

It wasn't the first time, that's why their neighbor Tursunoy was upset because of Dilbar's condition. It was difficult for this poor woman.
Tursunoy opa went outside and sat down at the table in front of the house and called Dilbar to her.

"I see your condition. You're sure to get sick! My advice to you as a sister is to sell your house and pay off your debts. If Komiljon is healthy, you will not be homeless. You can get out of these things. Don't pay attention people's different ideas. Dilbar seemed to like her words.
"I will try to talk to my husband," she said while wiping her tears.
"This is too much for you. Don't be too nervous! You'll forget all about this!" Difficulty and deprivation had greatly bent Dilbar's body. That's why she didn't want anyone to ask about her feelings. If somebody asked such questions, she would feel as if her soul was crying. She looked at those around her with envy. When she saw the smiling women, she used to get saddened.
When Dilbar told to Kmiljon Tursunoy opa's words, he thought.
"If we sell the house, we will stay on the street! What about the children? We can't do it."
"Okay, the father of my children, let's say we don't sell it, but how can we pay off our debt? You can hear what the debtors are saying. Let's sell the house and pay the debts. Let's live in peace even if we live in a rented house."
Komiljon liked Dilbar's next words. That was the truth.
The next morning, he found one or two of those who were looking for a house. They told the buyers everything as it was. They turned out to

be conscious buyers and said, "Okay, I'll pay for the house, but we don't need a house right now. Until then, you can go on living in it. I also need sawab." Dilbar was really happy to hear that and said, "Thank you, I will not forget your kindness!" She could not contain her joy.

The buyers who came in the morning saw the house and estimated it at 60,000 soums. In desperation, Dilbar had no choice but to say "OK". In the afternoon, they counted the money and handed it to Komiljon.
"Now you can live here comfortably. My nephew who bought the house works in the desert. He will not come in two or three years," she added. After seeing off the owners of the house, Dilbar took the money to the debtors on the same day. After getting rid of a lot of debts, she felt a little calmer.
"We sold the house now," said Dilbar, "let's save money to buy another house. We'll have to work harder. You should also try to find a job."
"How do I go out? There is no one left who has not heard," said Komiljon, "I will go to the post office tomorrow." They will help me with some sort of work," he added.
It was not easy to find a job so. He remained at home again. In the meantime, Dilbar went to the post office a couple of times. When there was no result, she wrote a letter to the Ministry of Communications of the Republic. It was

openly written that everything that happened was not her husband's fault, and that it was organized on purpose. Fifteen days later, Komiljon was called to the communications department and hired as a postman. Thanks to that, he started working again. Three months later, he was fired again because there was a defalcation, but this time they filed the papers as if he was relieved of his post of his own free will. Komiljon, who left his job with debts hanging around his neck, fell into a deep depression. He started drinking. There was not a single day he did not drink.

"There is no justice," he used to say.

"Get a hold of yourself," Dilbar's attempts were in vein. Komiljon, who gradually became unable to live without alcohol, could not see anything else. When he couldn't find money to drink, he took out whatever he could get from home and sold it, in order to get some vodka.

Hard times began again for Dilbar. On the one hand, Dilbar, who did not know what to do when the landlords came to repair the house, started looking for a house to rent again. Even though her children were young, they became helpers to Dilbar. She remembered her childhood when they began to earn a living by working at a car wash center. "They are like me! How can I bear it when they are raising a family while yet too young, when they should be studying and playing and laughing! Oh my

Creator! How can I bear this!" She used to wail like this every day. She felt humiliated seeing her children's wet clothes, and she was embarrassed that she could not make things better for them.

Months passed after days. Meanwhile, Dilbar found a house to rent and moved. They worked with their children, but what they earned did not exceed their living. In such difficult days, Dilbar's thoughts were only about earning money and buying a house, and it was not something that she could stop thinking about. Dilbar had nothing left to support her children. She even bought and sold things in the market, but the money she earned was not enough for anything. Meanwhile, her children could not even go to school. Dilbar was saddened that her children were also seeing the difficult times like she had seen.

Sometimes Dilbar would cry aloud without being seen by her children. She saw such difficult days that she did not even have anything to cook a meal with. She did not complain even in the days when she ate one loaf of bread for three days. She was ashamed to tell someone about her pain or ask for help. There was nothing at home that day. Dilbar will never forget it. Her second son went out to the meat market early in the morning (at that time, butchers used to buy cattle from the stock market and make them led home), but not a single butcher asked her son to lead any cattle that day. At lunch, her son came in with wet shoes. Seeing that there was no bread to eat, he went back to the market. The he saw a woman selling apples went to her and said, "Opa, how much will you give me if I sell all your apples?" She also said that she would give fifty soums without thinking. The boy immediately started to shout and praised the apple and quite soon sold all the apple. The woman, who was happy that her apples were finished, gave paid the boy and said to come next week too. He then happily brought home some oil, half a kilo of rice, carrots, four eggs and bread.

"Look, today we will also make pilaf," he said, unable to hide his joy. Even though Dilbar was crying inside, she was trying to show herself happy to her children.

Dilbar's heart was broken when she looked at her children, who were speaking about something. Now other kids of their age are watching TV at home. These are my poor children! Dilbar was again overwhelmed.

Without warning, she slowly entered the empty room and cried. She did not complain about her life. She only begged the creator, and she remembered the days of prosperity in her life.

They were already sitting at the table when

there was a knock on the door. Dilbar, who opened the door thinking it was one of the neighbors, was happy to see her former neighbor Tursinoy opa. The two talked for a long time. While putting the home-baked bread on the table with some pilaf in her hand, she put three hundred soums in Dilbar's hand, "Use it for food." Embarrassed, Dilbar couldn't help but say "Thank you!" If she had said anything else, she would have cried. Tursunoy opa noticed this, said goodbye and left. After she left, when Dilbar came to the table and saw that Komiljon was looking at his wife with pity, she immediately turned her eyes to her children. "Take it! It's hot!" The children also sat silently, seeing the sadness on their father's and mother's faces.

When the table was assembled Dilbar said, "The father of my children, I have to speak to you," she said. If I take one of the children and find a job in Tashkent, we would be in a better situation. I'm thinking on the kids. One of them hasn't got clothes, the other one shoes to wear. On top of that, the rent payment is coming up. I would earn and send money faster if you took care of the children. In this situation, we will suffer even more. Besides, we have a debt. Think about it," she said, and went out to do the washing up.

On the one hand, what Dilbar said was right

and she wants to do something for a living. What about me Instead of earning some money as a man... We have lost everything. Tears filled Komiljon's eyes, but trying to hide them from Dilbar, she got up and walked towards the balcony. Although the life cycle is the same, the worries of life are different. One has a sweet wedding anxiety, while another has a bittersweet one! Someone strives for another, and one strives to get rid of another, in order to get on a straight road. Dilbar was ready to do whatever it took to get rid of these bitter worries and live a better life with her family. First, they started selling tea in the Tashkent Hippodrome market, especially in the night market, hot tea was often requested. Fortunately for Dilbar, the landlord was a good person. He made all conditions for her to work, "You, my daughter, take action and be active, it will be fine," he said, understanding Dilbar's situation. Since there were many marketers in her house, she also prepared dinner for them. This way, they earned good money. One day, Dilbar was happy to see a woman who lived in the neighborhood next to them, "Sister, give this money to my children," she begged. The woman said "OK" and took the money. Two months later, the poor Dilorom went home for Kurban Bayram. She bought some clothes, a lot of food, and took some money for her children, but when she saw the condition of her children, she cried out loudly. The poor husband sometimes went hungry because he tried to make the money Dilbar had sent sufficient for a longer period. That day Dilbar suffered so much, she had never cried out loudly before, she cried with a severe pain in heart. In all these days, her parents-in-law or sisters-in-law had not come to them. There clothes were dirty. They themselves had become weak. Komiljon was suffering from fever in those days.

Because of this Dilbar had to stay at home again. Komiljon's condition was getting worse day by day. They went to every doctor and consulted them. All of them said one thing - Nervous! To tell the truth, we women, when we are very nervous, scream and shout and kill the pain. But men swallow the pain and increase the disease!
Not a day passed without troubles for Dilbar. She was trying to overcome all the problems which she considered to be the tests of the Creator. One day, Komiljon fell seriously ill. Frightened, Dilbar sent for his parents. But instead of his parents came his sister. Seeing her brother's condition, she started to shout at Dilbar, "It's you who put my brother in the situation." After all the time, the fact that her sister-in-law had not done anything for the wellbeing of Dilbar's family had a bad effect on Dilbar. She wanted to say something, but

caught sight of Komiljon, whose eyes were so sad, and stayed still. She didn't want Komiljon to suffer more, and put up with her words. The sister tried to take her brother, but Komiljon refused to go to his sister's place.

Dilbar was deeply worried about her husband's condition. Desperate, Dilbar went to the head of the neighborhood administration asking for help. Knowing the situation, the chairman added them to the aid money list for three months, but what would she do it. It won't be enough even for a week. But Dilbar was thankful for that.

After many days, Komiljon's temperature began to rise again. He wasn't enough strong even to walk. Dilbar took him to the doctor. She did not know what to do when the doctor examined him again and said that if he does not stay in the hospital, if he does not get treatment in time, his condition would get worse. She had no money for her husband's treatment at hospital, so she brought Komiljon back home. She was in a really difficult situation when she saw the landowher who was waiting for them at the door. Now, where will I find the rent money for them? It would be nice if they understand my situation, but what if they don't? What will I do if he starts shouting?! O God! Have mercy on your creature!

Dilbar, who had barely placed Kamiljon on the

bench in front of the house, said,
"Wellcome! We were not at home because I took my husband to the doctor. The rent was late because he has been ill. I am Sorry!"- Dilbar handed fifteen thousand soums from her bag as rent. The landlord said "I needed money" and took the money and left without saying a word. Dilbar's heart was so full that she was ready to cry out loudly if her husband was not sick, but she thought of Komiljon and swallowed her pains.

That day, when her children were sitting on the table during dinner, without telling their father, Dilbar cried to her children.
"How long will we suffer like this? We have no income from anywhere! I can't work. If we don't put your father in the hospital, he won't recover! My children, I'm dizzy! I paid the rent today. The second son who saw her mother in tears said, "Mom, I want to go to work in a bakery with my friend in Tashkent. Don't cry. Everything will be fine! We will also have our own house! Let my father get well first, but Dilbar was heartbroken to see that her husband was getting worse instead of getting better. Dilbar went out that night, unable to sleep. She sat staring at the stars for a while. She did not even notice her neighbor who approached her because she was lost in the dream as if she was talking to the stars.

"You looking up at the sky for so long?" said Makhbuba opa.

"Yes, sister, I'm obsessed! I didn't notice you."
"Well, you are not calm either. Is your husband okay?" Mahbuba asked that question and then was embarrassed.
"Yes, sister, I took him to the doctor today. I can't sleep. If I tell you I can't go to bed!" Suddenly Dilbar started crying. Mahbuba felt uneasy when for asking that question. "I will tell you a medicine. Try it, she said. Take one aspirin, divide it into four parts and give hip one part before going to bed every day. Give it ten days. It will heal him, inshaAllah. A relative of mine got recovered this way.

"May your wishes come true, sister!" Two neighbors talked for a long time. When leaving, Mahbuba opa reminded the remedy again.

Whether it was because of that remedy or Dilbar's nightly crying prayers reached God, her husband's condition got better day by day. His face was not pale anymore and he began to walk freely in the yard. It is true that pain is a guest. When God heals, the pain gradually goes away. Komiljon could stand up and walk in a month. Now Dilbar started looking for work again. Now even when her husband was good, she could not leave Komiljon and go far. Therefore, she found a day job in the market. There was help in every way.

It is impossible not to see the signs of the Creator who determines the destinies of people. Dilbar walked through different paths of life – sometimes wide and straight, sometimes narrow and crooked. Dilbar also suffered a lot of hardships and humiliation during her life, but she tried to overcome all of them with patience and endurance. But when one was overcome, the other would appear. Until she found a solution to one problem, another problem would arise.

On the day, Dilbar could not calm down and walked along the Ferghana canal for a long time. She sat looking at the water as if the water in the canal felt her pain. She then again walked far along the canal. She cried out all the pain in her heart. Nobody saw and heard her. Only the water seemed to flow taking away all her pain. By the time Dilbar turned back, the day was coming to its end. She felt somewhat relieved. As if there is no evil left in her heart. It was like the water carried away her sorrow.

After six years of such difficult and hard days, she reached brighter days. In the meantime, she went to work in Russia two or three times. Even then, her children accompanied her. A man does not die because of work. Dilbar worked hard without sparing herself. She was not afraid of cold or heat in order to have her own house. She was with her children. And Komiljon built a house. She turned the yard into a beautiful garden. She slowly began to see the joy after difficult days. Both Dilbar and Komiljon were proud of themselves. Their children grew up to be smart, kind children because they saw their parents through many hard times. Four daughters-in-law were brought to their house. They were seen and treated as their own daughters. At the time they were grandparents to eight grandchildren.

It was not said in vain, "The nose of a poor person starts bleeding when moth starts eating a meal." Now, when they were planning to retire, Komiljon suddenly passed away at the of 63. Now Dilbar's dreams have turned into dreams again.

Even though it had been difficult, she missed those days. Even a piece of hard bread had been tasty as she had had someone to lean against. Dilbar cried a lot after Komiljon passed away. "Your spouse is your life partner and your support," says Dilbar. A person who corrects your mistakes, helps and advises you is your lifelong companion. Dilbar, while sitting in the yard at night, looked at the distant sky and looked at the twinkling stars. It seems as if the soulmate is smiling from afar. While wiping her tears, she said, "May your soul rest in peace, dear father of my children!!!" said Dilbar, looking up at the stars.

***Havaskhan Kamchieva (Olimova)*** *in Kyrgyzstan in 1959, Ush region in the family of a farmer in Aravon district was born in 1966 in the district Admission to the 1st grade of Alisher Navoi schooli in 1976,she graduated from school in the 10th grade. In 1977, she went to Tashkent,to go to the state university of culture entered her poem training breeding began to take shape in 1983 Markhamat started his career in the district central library Since 2009, Markhamat district government "Soglom Avlod" charity work in the position of Chairman of the fund.*

*Currently, she is working as a promoter of spiritual and educational work in secondary school No. 43 in the district.Kyrgyzstan has been continuing its work along with it Member of Writers Union Kazakhstan.*

*She is also a member of the Writers' Union Uzbekistan Turan international writers, The real member of the Academy is a poetess,mother of five children, grandmother of ten grandchildren.*

www.ingramcontent.com/pod-product-compliance
Lightning Source LLC
LaVergne TN
LVHW021239080526
838199LV00088B/4754